The Collective

By William R. Herr

The Collective

Copyright © 2012 by William R. Herr

ISBN-13: 978-1479366712
ISBN-10: 1479366714

Dedication:

For Rob, Vince, Syd, Meghan, Corinne, Zach, Tara, Mark, Sean, and Super-Siuz. Please try not to blow yourselves up.

With special thanks to Monica Speca, whose dedication to the content was seconded only by her love of the oxford comma.

Table of Contents

Introduction

"Collective fear stimulates herd instinct, and tends to produce ferocity toward those who are not regarded as members of the herd."--**Bertrand Russell**

I did not begin with the goal of writing this book.

Initially, I began this project as an exercise to digest *The Crowd: A Study of the Popular Mind* by Gustave Le Bon, to supplement my own study of the dynamics of collectives. His work is very dense and written in the parlance of the late 1800's, and thus requires a bit of updating in order to comprehend it. This project was simply a way of updating it within my own mind, analogous to my own studies and experience. There were problems, however.

I was not through the first chapter before I realized that the work would require changes if it was to be both accurate and topical. Some assumptions of the late 19th century were completely false, as we now comprehend them. Others would convince the reader to discount all of his work, based on the prejudices of the time. The language was not necessarily archaic, but it was inaccessible to the degree that discussion of passages required significant paraphrasing. Examples were taken from French history, which was recent to Le Bon, but would seem nearly medieval to the modern reader. There were numerous passages in which Le Bon digressed into lengthy diatribes concerning the state of politics, philosophy, education, etc. Somewhere within that first chapter, I found that I was rewriting and updating his work for others and not for myself.

Almost immediately I found that I was inserting my own observations as well. Such observations might not be entirely mainstream in their content, but they work well in the study of collectives. I therefore let them stay and built on them. Such observations build on the work of William Wheeler and Emile Durkheim, although they are not bound to their philosophies. Great thinkers such as Vladimir Vernadski and H. G. Wells have expanded on the same subjects, but again my work is not tied to their concepts. Indeed, one can link their observations on the collective human race directly to Gustave Le Bon and the work which is here updated.

Chief among my additions has been the concept of the Collective Mind--not a new-age concept, but rather a way of explaining the function of individual organisms which band together to form a new organism. One need not consider that the collective mind exists as anything other than an abstraction any more than one need believe that the soul exists as more than an abstraction in order to understand the concept. One need only follow the actions of collectives, note their commonalities, categorize appropriately, and forward hypotheses based on the preceding work. To assist with comprehension, both for myself and for others, I developed a number of definitions, laws, and principles which I found applied to collectives regardless of their nature. I have introduced them in the text, and use them throughout.

To me, the most interesting aspect of the philosophy of Gustave Le Bon is that, even considering his prejudice and misogyny, his ideas work. As has often been said of quantum physics, even though we cannot definitively prove its assertions, we cannot ignore the fact that the principles of the study work when applied. The computer on which I wrote this book would not function if the principles of quantum physics were not valid and applicable, and likewise history has provided proof that Le Bon was brilliantly accurate. The rise of Mussolini in Italy can be traced in part to Le Bon, and he reportedly slept with a copy of *The Crowd* by his nightstand. Hitler studied his work in detail, and its effect can be seen in his repressive regime. Le Bon's fingerprints may be seen on communist China, Castro's Cuba, and in the rise and fall of political parties within the United States and across Europe. The ideas simply work. It is thus more of a pity that his writing is not more widely read.

If the information contained within *The Crowd* has been used to such damage throughout the world, why would one update it? That is a tough question, but it deserves to be asked. The concepts presented within both Le Bon's and this book are not intended to be a primer for world domination, although they have been used in that manner by the unscrupulous. They represent a method of understanding large collectives, and how they might be manipulated. That includes the understanding of how to resist such manipulation as well. Knowledge is neither good nor evil. Knowledge is. Good and evil might utilize knowledge for their own ends, to achieve those aims which they find important, but such action does not taint the knowledge. One need not utilize the knowledge within to benefit from it. If one understands how he is being manipulated, such manipulation is more apt to fail than to succeed. The information within these pages may be used as a metaphorical pair of X-ray glasses to see through the clothing of society. Motivations are laid bare, and the supposed subtlety of one's leaders is exposed for the fumbling attempts that normally predominate.

On a related subject, I should note that a large portion of this work is not my own. It is mostly the work of Gustave Le Bon, as translated by an unknown hand and distributed via Amazon.com over the Kindle platform. It includes insights gleaned from another of his works, *The Psychology of Revolution*. Burkheim was a large influence, as was Maslow (upon whose ideas I have relied heavily). It is updated with examples from present society and my own years of personal study, and adapted for comprehension, but in the end I cannot claim it. If I were to claim any level of ownership of this work, it would have to be as a ghost-writer or contributing author. Parts of this book are taken in whole-cloth from Le Bon's writing. Parts have been deleted entirely as redundant or demonstrably false—a fine example of this is a chapter on electoral collectives which not only duplicated conclusions found elsewhere, but spent a large portion of its time discussing the supposed failed premises of the Women's Suffrage movement. Other parts are mere paraphrases of his thoughts; many parts are wholly my own. In all cases I have struggled to preserve his authoritative voice rather than overbear it with my own.

It is my suggestion that this work should be read concurrently with the original, and with the understanding that the racism and misogyny of the 19th century do not detract from the content. It is my sincere hope that Le Bon would not disapprove of my treatment. Beyond this, there is little more to say.

Eat this book. Chew it and savor its bitter flavor. Digest it and make it part of your being. Welcome to the collective.

Chapter I: The Collective

"Dispassionate objectivity is itself a passion, for the real and for the truth."--**Abraham Maslow**

What is a collective? As the word is used here, a collective is a group of individuals with something in common which allows them to identify with each other. Initially, this might seem too broad a definition for effective study, but with rational observation one may draw some startling conclusions. If collectives are representative of their constituent individuals, then each collective should be as different as a single snowflake is different from another. To a degree this is true. However, regardless of the differences collectives, like snowflakes, are very much alike in very fundamental ways.

Consider the example of the snowflake. A single flake of snow is comprised of crystallized water which forms into a complex three-dimensional lattice. An exhausting study of individual flakes of snow might result in an understanding of the internal principles which cause crystals to form in a given fashion, or to deviate from the standard generation, or to fail to form at all. One might even develop a science around the study of such flakes[1], to categorize their individual archetypes and establish norms. Such study, however, would completely miss the fact that snow, when packed into a tight sphere and hurled at an opponent, will impact against a skull with a satisfying splat.

This is a book dedicated to an explanation of collectives: how they are formed, how they are controlled, and how they develop, how they think, and how they die. The entirety of the experience of a group, race, faction, or other designated large collection of people combines to form a collective personality, what Gustave Le Bon called "the genius of the race."[2] However, when a portion of those individuals form themselves, either through chance or by design, into a sub-group for any given purpose careful observation will show that they will exhibit new characteristics which may very well be in complete opposition to their original and individual character traits. In popular literature, the collective is considered brutal, murderous, and barbaric. Yet at the same time it may show inspired courage, lofty ideals, or unexpected restraint. To understand the nature of a collective, to predict its course, and to control that course requires an in-depth understanding of the underlying factors which contribute to the same. Once that understanding is met, the collective

---

1   It should be noted here that a Vermont farmer named Wilson Bentley did, in fact, attempt to build a science out of the study of snowflakes. In 1931 he published a book entitled, *Snow Crystals* which outlined the results of his exhaustive study. His work in capturing and photographing the crystals was published by many scientific journals and his photographs were collected by colleges and universities world-wide. He died as he lived, a Vermont farmer who rarely entered the halls of academia.

2   Gustave Le Bon, *The Crowd, A Study of the Popular Mind*

may be turned, released, dispersed, or gathered depending on its nature and the skills of its leadership.

Collectives have always been important to the growth and maintenance of nations and races. However, this importance gains significance at times when societies find themselves in flux--when nations' borders are redrawn, when wars arise, when ideologies shift or are cast aside, or when great concepts are implemented among often discontent populations. The subversion of individual motivations to the shifting desires of a collective may rightly be considered to be a leading hallmark of the current age, as will be seen throughout this book.

In order to understand the nature of collectives, however, one must be willing to step aside from their own. To view a collective from the perspective of an opposing viewpoint is a siren's trap: deceptively alluring, yet potentially deadly when the observed information is used to affect the collective in question. No individual exists without the influences of their own society, and no person can consider themselves purely unbiased. Just as our minds seem hard-wired to follow the strongest father-figure, so too our minds will accept or reject information based not on logic or fact, but based upon methods of reasoning and abstract images which have been impressed upon us from birth. One need not reject their own ideology to discover truth, but it is essential that one set it aside so that empathy and understanding of often competing ideologies may take place. This is the most viable method available to any individual to arrive at some semblance of truth, especially when dealing with questions of great controversy and passion.

One should also be wary about meddling with the structure of collectives, as their nature often depends in great part upon their mode of communication. A collective of elected officials, for instance, will have a nature dependent upon their mode of access to their constituencies and separate from the nature of a crowd of protesters; yet they will exhibit many of the same tendencies, follow the same laws of nature, and travel the same course through their collective's lifetime. The reason for this is that collective personalities exhibit much the same nature as individual personalities. They do not change suddenly without fracture. Nature often forces crises and sudden change upon collectives which forces change upon their character, yet the collective will strive to return to its original organization (or, failing that possibility, to match it as closely as possible). This explains why there seems nothing more fatal to a people than the passion for great reforms, regardless of the benefits these reforms might bring. Examples of this can be seen in the attempted transformation of the Afghan people, first by Russia and then by the U.S., and their inevitable return to a tribal nature. Only time and the will of the collective may change this nature, and even then almost always by near-imperceptible degrees.

Collectives are ruled by custom, beliefs, and ideas--matters which are the essence of their constituent individuals. Their institutions and laws reflect this character and express its needs. That a theocratic government might be found offensive to western society does not change its happy acceptance by Muslim society, nor do the legal institutions of western society bear any greater validity than those of the Far-East. They are expressions of their creators' racial identities, and their acceptance relates their utility in their respective arenas. A change in the social structures of a collective would not, therefore, change its character and would be quickly replaced by the very institutions which were removed.

The consideration of the organizational elements of a collective cannot be separated from that of the people and institutions from which it rose. Their existence has an absolute value, even if their function is of relatively little value. To understand the social value of institutions, one must view them, as it were, from multiple sides to understand their full import. One must have an empathic understanding of the individuals within the collective to fully understand the value of the created institution. In this way, one might approach truth rather than supposition.

To quote Gustave Le Bon:

> *"From the point of view of absolute truth a cube or a circle are invariable geometrical figures, rigorously defined by certain formulas. From the point of view of the impression they make on our eye these geometrical figures may assume very varied shapes. By perspective, the cube may be transformed into a pyramid or a square, the circle into an ellipse or a straight line. Moreover, the consideration of these fictitious shapes is far more important than that of the real shapes, for it is they*

11

and they alone that we see and that can be reproduced by photography or in pictures. In certain cases there is more truth in the unreal than in the real."[3]

When studying a collective, one should bear in mind that actions and institutions have a practical value which far exceeds any assumptions one might have as to the actual value. The western observer might conclude that the harshness of Sharia law makes it unwieldy and inhumane — thus without real value. This would be a correct assumption, were it imposed on Western society. However, Islamic societies welcome the law as a necessary extension of their character and nature. To enforce Western-European law would be equally inhumane.

Any study of collectives should also avoid the pitfall of over-analyzation. In any given society, there are endlessly shifting alliances, collectives in growth, and collectives in decline, institutions under construction, and institutions in decline. While careful observation might allow the focused individual to accurately quantify all variables in this social equation, the state of the society would change before the data was fully analyzed. Instead, an observer should allow that laws of chaos apply to all forms of life. It is through the application of certain laws and principles of collectives — truths which are invariable or very rarely vary — that one may be reasonably certain of outcomes; even then one may fully underestimate the underlying forces with which he might meddle.

---

3 Gustave Le Bon, *The Crowd, A Study of the Popular Mind*

While collectives are generally driven by the basest of instincts, they are often capable of actions which have in the past been considered destiny or the providence of God. Examples of this may be found in celebrated military victories and the rise of nations. The battle of Thermopolae was not simply a stunning example of Spartan obstinacy or the favor of the Greek gods—it was an excellent example of two groups which remained true to their collective soul in spectacular ways. Had Napoleon not risen to power, France's empirical aspirations likely would have vaulted another to supreme rule. While America considers its preeminence within western society to be divine providence, one must also conclude that its power derives at least equally from a national design which allows mobility between its competing constituent collectives. In each of these cases, the success or failure of the groups in question depends more upon the will of the collective than the will of the leadership.

One cannot always understand the causes of such events, and as will be shown such understanding is often unnecessary. We cannot, however, ignore their existence. Collectives seem, to the untrained eye, to move in random manner and to be subject to any whim. To the trained eye, however, they are susceptible to certain stimuli, and nearly immune to most others. They move not at random but according to predictable patterns, as if performing a dance without scope or form. While one might not accurately predict the direction that dancers might travel, he can understand the steps of the dance. While one might understand the direction, he cannot understand the steps. Not even the dancers can predict both at once.

If one desires to remain within the relative safety of available truth, and not to wander blindly through mazes of often-incorrect conjecture, he should examine the outward manifestation of the collective and accept this as truth regardless of any objections his reason might offer. One can only observe, form a hypothesis based on those observations, and then test the hypothesis through predictions or direct action upon the system in question. To adjust the hypothesis based on intuition might occasionally yield success, but far more often can result in the often deadly and bloody results found when exercising one's curiosity with high explosive.

Every value-assessment one makes about any particular collective is, as a rule, automatically false. Behind those actions one can observe are motivations which cannot be observed. To quote Donald Rumsfeld:

> *"There are known knowns; there are things we know we know. We also know there are known unknowns; that is to say we know there are some things we do not know. But there are also unknown unknowns--the ones we don't know we don't know."*[4]

---

4   United States Secretary of Defense Donald Rumsfeld, Press Briefing, Feb. 12, 2002

Chapter II: An Age of Dissolution

"No advance in wealth, no softening of manners, no reform or revolution has ever brought human equality a millimeter nearer."
– **George Orwell**

To understand how collectives act, one should understand the influences which cause them to act. Collectives are rarely moved by physical stimuli but instead by ideas. Religious institutions, political institutions, and rational institutions, and even the general state of such institutions as marriage and family are ingredients which contribute to the nature of a collective. Given the correct composition and prepared in the correct way, the collective becomes a volatile mixture which requires the mere lighting of a match to set it in motion.

We find ourselves, at the time of this writing, in an age of dissolution. Those foundations which Western society once considered sacrosanct and inviolable such as the Christian church, the court system, and national symbols, are subject to question, doubt and often near-hatred. It is at times such as these that the power of collectives is most explosive. One might accurately compare the present state of society to the late history of the Roman Empire. At first glance, the actions of the individual collectives could be considered as caused by the actions of a very few individuals with either gifted intelligence or great and secret power; yet no human intelligence, no matter how great, could accurately and expertly guide collectives in the directions they currently travel. To understand the forces at play, one must first accept that not everything can be controlled. Many times, coincidence is just that—random chance. At other times, what appears to be coincidence is actually the manifestation of the collective personality as it acts upon its environment. In very rare cases gifted internal or external leadership might be found to have acted upon collectives to produce desired results. However, most often the suspected individuals are unwitting slaves to their respective collectives. This is the danger of meddling in the affairs of motivated groups: assimilation and loss of perspective.

Upheavals within society do not begin with action. Action is a symptom of change and not a cause. Actions might trigger change as a catalyst however it is not effective if conditions are not prepared in advance. The true instigators of change are the currency of collectives: ideas and social status. From biblical accounts to current history, the grand advances in human society have been caused by invisible changes in human thought and perceived disparities in wealth. The reason these changes are relatively rare is that the underlying thought-processes of a collective are inherently stable.

Two major factors contribute to our current age. The first is the rejection of political, religious, and social bastions upon which our society is based. The second is the creation of new societal norms to meet the whims of the shifting collectives of our age. Because the rejected edifices of society still retain a portion of their former power and absolute value, and because the competing collectives are neither fully formed nor stabilized, the direction of change (or return to the former norms) has not yet been determined. It is during these times that an understanding of collectives is most important. Quoting Gustave Le Bon:

> *It is not easy to say as yet what will one day be evolved from this necessarily somewhat chaotic period. What will be the fundamental ideas on which the societies that are to succeed our own will be built up? We do not at present know. Still, it is already clear that on whatever lines the societies of the future are organized, they will have to count with a new power, with the last surviving sovereign force of modern times, the power of crowds. On the ruins of so many ideas formerly considered beyond discussion, and today decayed or decaying, of so many sources of authority that successive revolutions have destroyed, this power, which alone has arisen in their stead, seems soon destined to absorb the others."*[5]

Viewed from afar, the Information Age seems more an age of revolution and contagion. The transition of the Third World countries from states of a tribal nature to states of intellectual upheaval represents a shift in economic power as much as a change in status. With education comes the yearning for advancement. When yearnings are stifled

5 Gustave Le Bon, *The Crowd, A Study of the Popular Mind*

by lack of opportunity (or hoarding of opportunity) the result is an angry collective. If a collective is present, and motivated to action, it requires the barest of excuses to spring into immediate revolt.

The growth of the power of the masses begins at first with the propagation of ideas which are constantly repeated, implanting themselves into individuals' minds. Afterward, gradual association of those who wish to implement such ideals is inevitable. It is by association that collectives have come to adopt ideas which support their interests—ideas which are clearly defined, if not altogether just—and have become conscious of the strength of their numbers. As communication spreads, governing bodies fall before them. Outcomes such as these are predictable as well as avoidable. However, governing bodies rarely possess the creativity and intelligence (being collectives themselves) to direct collectives which might otherwise cause their destruction.

The demands of the collectives, currently, seem to be nothing less than the utter eradication of their societies' current structures. These demands, however, can be summarized as demands for justice which has, to the collective mind, been denied. With their lack of adaptation to reason, collectives are quick to act. As a result of their often loose organization, they are strong and difficult to eliminate. They do not comprehend that their demanded ideals will quickly become the ideals they sought to replace, and it would little matter if they did. In the end they wish to trade slave master for slave master, in the hope that the whippings will be less severe.

The church, once a bastion of respect, has become to a great number of individuals a matter of disdain. Successive scandals excited the mind of the collective to the point that resolution to alternate religions became preferable to continuation under what was considered a corrupt organization. Had the excesses belonged to one sect, the effect might not have been as severe. However, given the depth of disillusionment of the collective, all of Christianity—even those divisions which have been innocent of any wrongdoing—has become suspect. That this happened at a time of expansion within Islam and Wicca could be considered an aforementioned coincidence, or the circumstances might more rightly be attributed to a common cause. Regardless, to specify the cause, or lack thereof, would be to form conclusions based on likely incomplete data. The causes are therefore unimportant to the current situation. Causes cannot be changed, as their time has passed. Only future causes may be avoided, and repairs may be made to any edifices which have been damaged in the past by storms of excess.

The wide and omnipresent rock of capitalism, a collective in its own right, suffers from the excess of the past. As capitalism suffers, so the demand for socialism increases. Again we cannot reasonably ascertain with any surety whether these factors are linked by a common cause, and again any cause is now irrelevant except to ranks of historians. What is noted is that, as in remembered past, the mistakes of excess are met with mistakes of correction, which in turn are excess in their own right. Well regarded laws of economics are ignored in favor of expeditious repair, even though such repair must eventually cause greater harm. To replace such a system with another might now be possible, but without a knowledge of the methods to control economic collectives, any new system would likewise be doomed to failures as crises inevitably stacked against each other. As will be shown later in this work, such eventualities are the predictable result of parliamentary and congressional governments.

Once-stable dictatorships have been overthrown in favor of nebulous promises of freedom and democracy. One might argue that not all democracies are free, and that not all elected officials are honorable, yet for the first time in a very long time change comes to the Middle-East not through external force, but through internal variation of the ideals of society by a hopefully enlightened populace. Such change is the only form of lasting change possible within a collective, and thus the greatest hope for anything which the Western World might consider civilization. Of the hopes and aspirations of the citizens of the Middle Eastern countries, we can only guess. Yet one would assume that the approval of Western society would be among the lowest of their priorities.

A great deal of distrust has been generated among the masses for the once near-holy regard for science. With the demagoguery of popular expert opinion, the practice of discussion and dissent has been quashed until competing hypotheses must face each other not within the arena of logic but across the aisles of political parties. The end goal of scientific argument has ceased to be the arrival at truth, and instead the victory of argument regardless of truth. Because of this adversarial internecine combat, neither hypothesizer nor skeptic may regard their positions with any level of certainty once the argument has ended. If certainty cannot be had, then the arguments cannot cease.

In all of this, the masses have rejected the gods of their fathers—dictatorship and mother church, economic stability and scientific truth—in favor of gods of their own fashioning. Now is the time of dissolution for failed philosophy, and the adoption of new ideals. One can only hope that expert guidance allows that the newest failures will be improvements upon the former.

Throughout this historic process, the power of the collectives reigns supreme. Across the earth, regardless of nation, we see their symptoms and rise as they compete against each other and develop depth of personality. While we cannot stop such balkanization from occurring, we can guide such collectives through careful leadership. The question we must ask ourselves is, "Should we?" Should collectives be allowed to develop as fate and their constituency provides, or should they be guided in their course by those whose external viewpoint allows a greater breadth of vision? Questions such as these are beyond the scope of this text, and will not be answered here. However, to find such answers one must understand the collectives first.

Collectives do not only destroy. They can as easily create substance from a void, or bring music without instrument. Civilizations begin first as a barbarian phase which consists of incompletely formed and competing collectives, and this stage of history should expect no difference. It is with the evolution of a collective into a nation or fully-formed civilization that fixed rules, discipline, and a passing from instinctive action to rational action and forethought are possible. Collectives cannot achieve these goals on their own. Such goals must be the result of leadership within the collectives which guides them to greatness.

Only through insight into the nature of the collective can it be understood how immune they are to laws and institutions, how powerless their constituencies are to resist those ideals and opinions which are forced upon them, and that neither logic nor reason may appeal to them. Rather, they must be impressed with power and seduced by pleasure.

For instance, should a politician who wished to impose a new tax choose that which would be the most fair? Reason suggests that this would be best received, but reason would be wrong. In practicality, an unjust tax which affects the fewest individuals would be preferable to a fair tax whose burden is less, but shared equally. The politician would impress upon the mind of his constituency the power of taxation, and could point to the collective benefits such taxation would offer. While the unjust tax might raise the ire of a few, the fair tax would raise the ire of all. Given that the first impetus of any politician is to retain power, this is exactly what one would expect from any democratic process (although exceptions do apply). Consumption taxes (also known as sales taxes) likewise are considered less burdensome than property taxes, as the pennies taxed on all individuals might be accepted as a necessary use of political power while again the proceeds might be offered as a mutual benefit. A property tax which is levied once yearly, however, would seem overwhelming in scope to the collective. Such has been the case in the past, and such will be the case in the future.

Effective politicians have an innate understanding of the psychology of collective motivation and use that knowledge to their benefit. An understanding of the methods by which a collective may be motivated is not occult science or forbidden knowledge. Through the application of simple laws and principles any motivated group may be affected for good or ill. Economic collectives and political parties, protest groups and businesses, and even nations and alliances will respond equally to the same methods. With that realization history ceases to be a study of facts but rather a study of how such laws and principles have been used by the idealistic and the unscrupulous.

Chapter III: How the Pot is Stirred

"Ninety-nine per cent of the people in the world are fools and the rest of us are in great danger of contagion." – **Thornton Wilder**

Collectives are affected much differently than mobs. A mob is generally a gathering of individuals with little in common other than location, regardless of the chances which caused them to be in company. A mob might be a group of random shoppers in a mall, a group of commuters on a train, or visitors to an amusement park. While the constituents may share a common interest, they do not necessarily think or act alike. While a mob might be excited by circumstance into sudden action, or interested as a group by a well-timed display, it might just as easily wander aimlessly and without shared purpose. Its individual members exhibit no change in their nature, and are as likely to leave the mob as to remain with it. This text is interested in mobs only as they evolve into collectives.

Under certain circumstances a mob may evolve into an organism which exhibits new characteristics very different from those of the individuals of which it is composed. The mental state of the persons within the mob takes on the same direction, and the conscious personality disappears. A collective mind has been formed, which presents very clearly defined characteristics. One might well consider that the mob has evolved into a separate, single conscious being, and it exhibits a strikingly uniform personality.

How is a collective formed, then? A collective need not share location; communication and a common ideal or belief are necessary, but little else. The collective of the movement labeled "Occupy Wall Street" began not as a crowd of gathered individuals, but as a concept forwarded by a largely unknown Canadian agitator[6]. Certain conditions, which will be explained within this chapter, created a ripe environment for collective creation, not the least of which were:

1) Perceived comparative social status

2) Contagion

3) Suggestion of romantic history

Given these factors, the desire for action was present and palpable. The sole necessity for the formation of the collection was a seductive concept which captured the popular imagination. As frustration over social pressures increased, and example collectives formed elsewhere, the suggestion of forming an occupying force within the major cities of nations gained a romantic allure which hearkened to the oft-romanticized protests of the 1960's. Propagation of the concept occurred over the Internet, and spread

---

6   The Canadian magazine *Adbusters* initially suggested the protests, and the concept has been attributed to Senior Editor Micah White.

world-wide.

In much the same way, the Tea Party collective was formed. In the case of the Tea Party, the imaginations of conservatives across the United States were excited by the shock of sudden economic failure and a fear of uncertain future. These excitations and fears where further propelled by both opposition and support within the media. It should be noted that collectives which are driven to action require an object, and the opposition to their formation provided that object. It should further be noted that the Tea Party, though it claimed to be leaderless, received ample leadership support through personalities within talk radio[7]--a condition which allowed them to uniformly maintain and enforce a standard of morals and self-restraint which is often not present in collectives.

An entire nation may devolve to become a collective, given the proper circumstances. Within the movement which later became known as 'Arab Spring', a popular majority rose to oppose dictatorial rule first in the nation of Tunisia, and then in Egypt. Following the attacks of September 11, 2001, the United States formed a single national collective. If one were to look in a more broad manner, one might consider that Western civilization joined into a collective following the attacks on the World Trade Center and Pentagon, or into two competing global

---

7 Although leadership was not vested in a single individual, it deserves to be noted that talk-radio host Glenn Beck almost daily extorted the Tea Party enthusiasts not to respond to violence with violence, and to peacefully eject individuals from their ranks who demonstrated values other than their own. In addition, he helped to provide organizational tools which allowed mental unity to propagate. Other notable figures who provided direction were Rush Limbaugh, Sean Hannity, Mark Lavine, and Michael Savage.

collectives following the fall of Poland to the Nazi regime prior to WWII.

Once formed, a collective acquires certain observable general characteristics. Beside these characteristics there are additional particular aspects which vary according to the nature of the individual constituents, and these may modify its collective mental nature. Upon careful examination one would find that organized collectives have much in common with disorganized collectives—that is, collectives composed of like-minded individuals as opposed to collectives composed of diverse elements. Between these two forms of collectives there are differences enough, however, that one may differentiate between them based on observation alone, and to a degree predict their progress.

Before one concentrates on the differences between collectives, he should understand those characteristics which collectives hold in common. It is not easy to describe the collective mind, as it is dependent upon common elements within the collective (even in diverse collectives), as well as the conditions of its formation. As the character of an individual changes with the addition of new experience, so too does the character of the collective mind change with the addition of new members. Just as an individual may, given a sudden change in situation, perform acts in opposition to his character, so too may members of a collective change character without notice, often in remarkable ways. During the protests of Tienanmen Square in China, otherwise inoffensive and compliant students exhibited amazing courage and tenacity, even in the face of certain destruction. Given any other circumstances, however, they might likely have eventually taken their place as citizens within the political party without incident.

Once a collective has reached sufficient organization, certain controlling actions take place. Ideas which might be individually considered foreign become repeated to the degree that they are accepted as fact. Language changes to reflect the new reality of the collective mind. Individuals within the collective willingly stop questioning, and assume the thoughts, aspirations, and hatreds of the collective.

The most striking characteristic exhibited by collectives is the *Law of Mental Unity*:

> *Regardless of the constituent individuals, and regardless of their differences, transformation into a collective endows them with a collective mind which makes them tend to feel, think, and act in a different manner than they would think, act and feel in isolation. This effect is identical for all individuals within the collective, and directly proportional to the strength with which they identify with the collective.*[8]

Likewise, and although it might appear counter-intuitive, the character of a collective will not be an aggregation or median level of the characters of the constituents. What actually happens is a combination,

---

[8] The laws and principles provided within this book are a product of my own observations and are not borrowed from other works. I offer them solely as a means of predicting the effects of applied collective dynamics.

followed by the creation of new characteristics, much as when vinegar is added to baking soda: the result is very different from the constituent ingredients.

Additionally, one will note that while the *Law of Mental Unity* is applicable to all members of a collective, it is often applicable in varying degrees between members. To understand this one must understand Maslow's motivational hierarchy which delineates human motivation. Maslow reasons that motivations have a hierarchy and that this hierarchy is identical for every human being. This text will therefore borrow from the work of Maslow in the presentation of the **Law of Collective Motivation**: *The susceptibility of the individual within any collective to the Law of Mental Unity is indirectly proportional to their perceived comparative status within Maslow's Hierarchy.*

Maslow's hierarchy of needs[9] basically shows that humans vary in their motives for action or inaction based on their underlying condition of existence. Individuals will progress through the hierarchy after having achieved each state for a progressively increasing duration.

According to Maslow, the base state for any individual is a survival mode, wherein the individual is motivated to secure the necessities of life such as food, water, shelter, and reproduction. Once these necessities are secured, next humans are motivated to ensure continuing access to these necessities: security of body, home, resources, employment, and morality. Once this condition

---

9   Abraham Maslow, "A Theory of Human Motivation"; Psychological
    Review 50(4) (1943)

has been met to a satisfactory degree, the individual progresses to be motivated to achieve social acceptance; he or she requires love, friendship, and sexual intimacy (as opposed to simple reproduction). Next the individual is motivated to actions which relate to esteem: self-esteem, the esteem of others, confidence, and achievement. Finally, having reached this plateau the individual is motivated to achieve self-actualization; the development of a moral code, creativity, spontaneity, elimination of personal prejudices, and problem solving, and an acceptance of reality.[10]

It should further be noted that the individual's actual status within the hierarchy is less important than their perceived status compared to others. An individual with all of the needs for life, ample security, acceptance within society, and ample self-esteem may still consider themselves at a lower state if they compare themselves to other classes within society. If this is the case, they will be more susceptible to the collective mind than others who might be oblivious to the status of their peers.

To understand the underlying causes for the power of *The Law of Mental Unity*, one must understand that unconscious motivations often play a stronger role in one's decisions than those of the conscious. Within the shifting and chaotic center of the collective, the individual is subjected to stresses which are absent from normal solitude. The ego withdraws, and survival instincts come to the fore. Chief among these is the urge to remain within the tribe, to

---

10 It should be noted that Maslow's theory was not the final treatment of the subject. The study of human motivations has been revisited by many psychologists. This has not stopped Maslow's version from being taught in the study of marketing and business.

gain the protection of numbers. To this end, the mind seeks the approval of one's peers and readily accepts the desires of the collective. Once this occurs, the unconscious becomes the conscious, and the conscious simply consults.

It is in the unconscious motivations of the members that the different elements of a collective resemble each other, while it is in their conscious minds that they differ. An uneducated day-laborer and a college professor, when joined together in a collective will find that their instincts, passions, and feelings are quite similar. It is sadly the case that while education might give fertile ground for high thought, it does nothing to differentiate character between two divergent individuals.

As an example of this, consider again the Occupy Wall Street movement. The crowds of protestors within the movement were not solely composed of malcontents and fringe-elements. Also present were protesters from widely different strata of society, including the unemployed, day-laborers, and executives. If a large number of these protesters did not participate in clashes with police this is more due to a failure on the part of the agitators rather than to a lack of mental unity.

Because of this rise of the subconscious, character within the collective becomes a common possession. Intellectual ability is weakened. Differences are overcome by commonalities, and the unconscious dominates the conscious. This explains why collectives can only with great difficulty accomplish tasks which require depth of thought. Decisions which are made by an assembly of experts in different fields will be of no greater value than those decisions made by delinquent children (indeed, the latter might easily be superior). Without commonality of experience, they can only share the basic qualities which are present in all individuals. In the collective, it is not intellect but instinct which aggregates.

If one were to study the individuals within a collective and list out the qualities shared by its members, one would expect to find an average and not what is actually the case—the creation of new characteristics. The reasons for this are easily understood, if not immediately obvious. The individual within a collective gains a numerical strength by association, which conveys the sensation of invincible power. This sensation allows the individual to yield to instincts which would otherwise be held in check. The individual will be less likely to restrain himself from action given the anonymity which the collective provides. To this end, any sense of responsibility disappears.

Additionally, collectives are subject to the *Law of Contagion*: *Stimuli within a portion of a collective will affect the entire collective.* Contagion can best be described as follows: when a member submits himself to the collective will, he becomes subject to each sentiment and act within the collective. The effect is much the same as hypnosis, yet without a hypnotist. In a collective contagion affects the individual to such a degree that he may very well sacrifice himself in the collective interest. This is an act which, in isolation, is most often considered heroic. In a collective, however, it is often involuntary.

Within a locally gathered collective, communication between individual members is near immediate through both verbal cues, such as speech, and visual cues. A flock of birds will whirl and turn in unison because their expectant attention immediately notes changes in flight and allows for adjustment so that the individual may continue to remain with the flock. Mass-media is effective to propagate contagion, as it communicates thoughts and ideas immediately to receptive viewers. Similarly, with the current ubiquity of the Internet, the capacity for contagion has over the past few decades increased exponentially. It should be noted that the contagion of the Tunisian uprising spread as a virus throughout the Muslim world due, in large part, to the existence of the Internet and the utility of both Facebook and Youtube.

Finally, and most importantly, collectives are subject to the **Law of Suggestibility**: *the collective mind is susceptible to suggestion in the same manner as a hypnotized subject.* While the *Law of Contagion* applies to internal sentiments and acts, the *Law of Suggestibility* applies to external stimuli. Once the subconscious has gained control of the personality, the individual is in much the same state as the subject of a hypnotist. From *The Art of Contrarian Trading: How to Profit from Crowd Behavior in the Financial Markets* by Carl Futia one may see an excellent example of this theory as applied to the financial world:

"A fascinating example of the suggestibility of stock market crowds developed during the late stages of the stock market bubble in the late 1990s. Companies with ".com" in their names were priced at a premium by the market, and several were motivated to change their corporate names for this reason. Of course, no value per se resides in a mere name, but the **image** *of a dot-com company was strongly associated with stock market profits. This made every such stock a favorite of the bubble crowds of the late 1990s. Similar things happen in every stock market boom and illustrate the important role that images play in investment crowds."*[11]

One will observe, therefore, that the uncontrolled unconscious results in the incapacity for independent thought, a unanimity of experience, and a susceptibility to suggestion which borders on hypnosis. The individuals within the collective, because of their expectant attention, assumed anonymity, and superiority in numbers, will have the tendency to immediately translate sensation and suggestion into action. These are the common characteristics of crowds regardless of their nature. The individual is no longer an individual, but rather might be considered a remote-control robot, a cellular extension of the will of the whole. Alone, the member might be a pillar of society. Within the collective, he bears little difference in personality from an uncontrolled child, with all of the possible barbarism and brutality that such a state implies.

---

11 Carl Futia, *The Art of Contrarian Trading: How to Profit from Crowd Behavior in the Financial Markets*, John Wiley & Sons, Inc.

It is wise, therefore, that collectives of townspeople within the United States are forbidden to form 'posses' or 'lynch mobs'. Their powers of reasoning are suspect because of their membership within the collective. Such a group would be just as apt to kill an innocent victim as to locate and punish a perpetrator. Following any such action, the individuals would be as likely to celebrate error as well as accurate success. To again quote Gustave Le Bon,

> *"It is not only by his acts that the individual in a crowd differs essentially from himself. Even before he has entirely lost his independence, his ideas and feelings have undergone a transformation, and the transformation is so profound as to change the miser into a spendthrift, the skeptic into a believer, the honest man into a criminal, and the coward into a hero."*[12]

While the intellect of the collective might be inferior, the feelings and motivations of the collective might very well be superior to that of the individual. Individually, none of the soldiers in the army of George Washington might have agreed to the privation of Valley Forge, much less the subsequent crossing of the Delaware River and successful attack upon the British forces. Likewise, in the Battle of the Bulge during WWII, an individual with no membership within the collective might more aptly have surrendered to the positionally superior German forces. However, strength in numbers and a sense of invulnerability (despite the intellectual understanding that death was very real and possible as an outcome) allowed

---

12 Gustave Le Bon, *The Crowd, A Study of the Popular Mind*

the return message of "NUTS!" to the German commander who solicited the terms of surrender.

Taken cumulatively, these laws are the basic implements necessary to create the explosive mixture. Like the beakers, burners, and glass-rods of a chemist's laboratory, they represent the tools with which elements may be caused to interact with each other. The tools are not enough, however. Any first-year chemistry student may be able to hold a beaker, yet that ability does not confer with it the understanding of how to create gunpowder. Given shelves of ingredients the novice might succeed in creating an explosive by adding the contents of random vials, yet such a neophyte will more likely create a stink-bomb, an inert mixture, or at worst destroy the laboratory in a premature explosion. To avoid this, he must next learn the proper ingredients, how to add them to the mixture, and the ways in which they might interact.

Chapter IV: The Chemical Properties of Unstable Elements

"Hypocrisy can afford to be magnificent in its promises, for never intending to go beyond promise, it costs nothing." – **Edmund Burke**

To recap, collectives are guided almost exclusively by the unconscious motives of their constituents. Membership within the collective grants the individual license to indulge in the more primitive of man's natural instincts; those which provided safety and continuity in earlier times of his existence. Alternatively, one might consider each collective to be an extended tribe or family, with all of the responsibilities and privileges such membership entails. Indeed, a tribe or family is a collective in its own right. The acts which are performed by the collective may be exquisite in terms of execution, but as they are directed by the basest of instincts, their execution is directed not by rationality but by those excitements dictated by the *Law of Contagion* and the *Law of Suggestibility*. As the collective is at the mercy of outside influences, and the rationality of the individual is subordinated to the whim of the unconscious, those impulsive reactions which might otherwise be repressed are released into action.

The actions of a collective may be, depending upon applied suggestion, either generous or cruel, heroic or cowardly, but they will be so dominated by the *Law of Mental Unity* that the interest of the individual will not vary them. As collectives exist ultimately within uncontrolled environments, and the possible suggestions are so varied, collectives become very unstable. This explains how it is that one might see an anarchistic collective pass from seeming bloodthirsty violence to generosity and heroism. The group might easily take the part of executioner, but no less easily might choose to martyr themselves to protect the innocent. Collectives are responsible through history for the ascendancy of belief, and are likewise responsible for the rivers of blood spilled in the acquisition of that ascendancy. It is not necessary to travel backwards very far through the annals of history to find examples of this. Following the attacks of September 11, 2001 upon the United States, the U.S. Armed Services received a wave of volunteers for service. That these individuals, now part of a national collective, were willing to voluntarily enter into life-threatening situations based on the emotion of the moment might seem unremarkable, until one considers that any of them, individually, would be less likely to do the same for the same collective had the attacks not happened. The shock of the attacks was the catalyst for nationalistic fervor, which translated itself to near immediate action.

Any suggestion of premeditation by a collective is therefore out of the question. Premeditation on behalf a collective is only possible through the effective use of leadership (discussed later within this text), in which the collective is used as a tool much the same way a chemist might apply flame to cause elements to interact, or shake a beaker to mix the contents. The collective might be excited in succession by conflicting sentiments, but always by the suggestion of the moment. They are willing sparrows in a hurricane, thrown in varying directions by forces which are beyond their understanding.

This instability renders them difficult to direct, especially when they gain control of a section of government. If the basic requirements of life did not require some sort of regulating leadership, most modern democracies would fall immediately into disrepair and collapse. Yet, while the unpremeditated sentiments of a collective are powerful and immediate, they do not last. Collectives are as incapable of accurate memory as they are of regulating their desires.

Collectives are not merely impulsive and unstable. The existence of the collective and its perceived numerical superiority relates to a sense of invulnerability for the whole. It is not prepared to admit that anything might block the path between desire and realization. It has no ability to understand that such intervention might exist. The concept of defeat disappears for individuals within the collective. The individual Chinese student might understand perfectly well that his voice cannot vary the intent of an entrenched leadership, yet that same student camped in protest in Tienanmen Square with every expectation that his efforts would be rewarded with success. While the students themselves were utterly defeated, their message caught the popular attention of the larger collective, and their message of individual freedoms eventually blossomed into reforms.

The fundamental characteristics of the group from which the collectives spring always exert an influence upon the nature of the collective. Collectives are, after all, not islands within a sea of influence. They exist within larger local collectives, which in turn exist within national collectives. The chain of collectives expands eventually to constitute the entire human race, which can be considered a disorganized, unmotivated collective. As has often been remarked, a sudden threat to the survival of the race might very well usher in a worldwide, if short-lived, organized collective. Both WWI and WWII could be considered clashes of global collectives. Europe, as diverse as it has always been and as constituted of such varying peoples, has repeatedly been ruled by a single collective: Alexander the Great, Rome, the Catholic Church, and more recently the European Union are effective examples which require no further extrapolation.

Thus, while a collective is almost always irritable and impulsive, these qualities exist to a greater or lesser degree depending upon the parent from which it hassprung. For instance, the difference between Occupy Wall Street and the Tea Party is striking, even though both movements seemingly sprang from the same parent group. It is when we examine the true nature of the parent that we see the reasons for the differences. While the Tea Party collective sprang from the loins of Christian conservatism, the Occupy Wall Street collective derived from the more liberal and diverse Progressive movement. Whereas the former held the institutions of law enforcement in high esteem, the latter held them in often blatant contempt. Thus, when protest ensued, it was the Tea Party collective which garnered peaceful success in the installation of representation within the governing body, while the Occupy Wall Street collective suffered repeated clashes with police.

As has been stated before, collectives are susceptible to the *Law of Suggestibility* and the *Law of Contagion*. Likewise, examples have been given as to the relative immutability of these laws. However indifferent to its surroundings a collective might appear, it is in a state of expectant attention. Suggestions which are offered to the collective are implanted into the subconscious of a portion of the constituents, and through contagion spread until the collective reaches mental unity.

As is the case with individuals, so is the case with the collective mind. A suggestion, once accepted, lends itself to immediate action dependent upon the cause. Whether the act is that of bloody uprising, as in the Libyan revolt of 2011[13], or the self sacrifice of the trucker fuel protests of 2005-06[14], the result is the same. There is little connection

---

13 While the Libyan uprising had its roots in the revolutionary past of the Qaddafi regime, it did not begin in earnest until a call for protest was published via the internet by writer and journalist Jamal al-Hajji. Once this suggestion was implanted in the Libyan collective it spread like wildfire and was a unifying force in a country with 20% unemployment and great disparities in perceived social status.

14 The trucker protests of 2005-06, led by figurehead Mark Kirsch and the hastily formed 'Truckers and Citizens United', were a fine example of how a disorganized collective may unify toward a specific purpose. Not even the participants in the protests agreed upon the basis of their anger, which revolved around the skyrocketing cost of diesel fuel, yet they were able to unify to the purpose of forming convoys on capital cities. Their lack of a

between the possibility of success and the acts which follow, nor does reason play any great part.

As collectives are constantly bordering on a state of unconscious action, readily yield to suggestions, and have the violence of individuals who have no recourse to reason, they cannot be anything other than excessively credulous. The perverse will seem common sense to the collective, and the greatest of contradictions might seem the most related of concepts. During the American Civil War, the concept that "all men are created equal" could exist side by side with slavery in the South. Similarly, the concept of States' Rights existed easily beside the idea of forced compliance in the North.

A sense of improbability does not exist for the collective. When faced with ranks of placid officers, a former Marine and participant in the Occupy Wall Street collective shouted, "There is no honor in this!" to them, as if they were in the process of an attack[15]. That there was no attack, nor had the police planned any action, was of no import. The emotional plea of the single protester gained traction across the Internet and the question became moot. The credulousness of the collective over-rode the lack of reason of the whole. Le Bon gives a similar example from

coherent unifying external leadership eventually resulted in dissolution and an end to the protests. While the protests generally involved, at their height, multiple hundreds of individuals, the shockingly loud display of large commercial vehicles captured interest both locally, nationally, and internationally, and provided additional suggestion for protests in the following years.

15 Sgt. Shamar Thomas, veteran of the 3rd Light Armored Reconnaissance Battalion proceeded to lecture the police officers who were present. As is usually the case, his speech was interpreted by different collectives based on the context of their collective personalities rather than actual intent.

the 19th century:

> *Persons who went through the siege of Paris saw numerous examples of this credulity of crowds. A candle alight in an upper story was immediately looked upon as a signal given the besiegers, although it was evident, after a moment of reflection, that it was utterly impossible to catch sight of the light of the candle at a distance of several miles.*[16]

The creation of fictitious images within the collective imagination is not solely due to the extreme credulity. It is also the result of an invariable side-effect to contagion: the degradation of message. A collective thinks in images, which call into being other related images, even though these images might have no connection to the primary. As demonstration, an individual might be called upon to record those images brought to mind by a suggestive idea. Given the initial concept of a princess, his mind creates a common fairy tale ideal. Then, immediately after, his mind will bring to bear other related images which have import to only his own mind: a horse, a knight, a castle, or the heaving breast of pubescent dreams. In succession, these images give rise to others, and still others, until the succession of his thought eventually leads him to concepts which are as foreign to the concept of a princess as a stone is to a rhinoceros.[17]

---

16 Gustave Le Bon, *The Crowd, A Study of the Popular Mind*

17 This process was first codified by Aristotle in *De Memoria et Reminencentia* and was later expanded by psychologists such as Thomas Hobbes and John Locke, among others.

Our reason shows us the incoherence of these images, and we can through use of reason accept or reject them as we see fit. The collective has no reason, and so cannot differentiate between imagination and reality. It accepts as real the abstract images evoked in the collective mind, even though they most often have only distant relation with the observed fact.

Given that collectives are composed of individuals who will perceive different facts differently, one might suppose that the perversion of reality would differ endlessly throughout the collective. However, again the *Law of Mental Unity* and the *Law of Contagion* arise to enforce the perversion of one, or some, on all. As a result of these two laws, the perversions are of the same kind. A classic example of this is an optical illusion involving two complex, mirrored designs. Upon first glance, it appears to be random shapes to the casual observer. However, if below we see the caption, "Do you see a vase or two women?" the observer will immediately understand and see both. The observer has, through communication, joined an invisible collective if only for the moment. In the future, when faced with such optical illusions, he will strive to find the 'secret design' almost without thinking. The picture was no more than an abstraction rendered by a cunning hand. After the communication it remained no more than cunning abstraction. The interpretation of the image changed; once changed, it remained accepted reality.

Perversions of truth, because they often seem miraculous or overtly shocking in some way, spread quickly through collectives. Such perversions have the authenticity of established fact as they are observed by multiple individuals. Because of this, or as a happy coincidence, mankind has established omnipresent modes of verification. When the Black Caucus was led past impassioned Tea Party protesters[18], a member of the caucus claimed to have distinctly heard the word "nigger" uttered by one of the protesters. Immediately the word was recalled by the other members of the collective, and the perversion implanted itself as a fact in that particular collective mind. Even though the entire process was recorded by multiple individuals from multiple angles, no recording of the supposed utterance was made. In this way one may discern truth as opposed to the collective experience, which may vary widely from fact. The intelligence of individual witnesses is not sufficient to combat this effect. Upon joining a collective, the doctor and the janitor are equally incapable of reasoned observation.

It is not necessary that a collective should be numerous for this effect to take place. As soon as a few individuals are gathered together with a common impetus they constitute a collective, and they assume the qualities and obey the laws of collectives regardless of their education with regard to areas outside of their specialty. Unless a specialty were shared by all present, likely any dissent from the collective mind would be quashed. This is the meat and bread of the illusionist. Despite acceptance that magical abilities such as teleportation and levitation are mere tricks, a collective audience will suspend their disbelief and see exactly that which the illusionist intends.

18 March 20, 2010, at the height of the health-care protests in Washington, DC, USA.

47

Alone, they might easily see through such trickery. As a collective, they are willing witnesses to miracles.

To return to the initial premise, collective observation is as perverse as possible, and most often simply represents an illusion which is observed by a single individual. Then through application of contagion, the illusion is shared through suggestion to others within the collective. This also explains why the media of different collectives will report opposing facts on a single story. The truth is not with one, or the other, but most often lost in a separate location altogether. From Le Bon:

> "Do we know in the case of one single battle exactly how it took place? I am very doubtful on the point. We know who were the conquerors and the conquered, but this is probably all."[19]

One must not place too great a confidence in the value of a collective's testimony. Unanimity of opinion as to the facts are not enough. Multiplicity of testimony is not enough. Without immutable recorded proof, there cannot be truth. Even with recorded proof, given the current level of sophistication in image manipulation, there cannot be surety of truth. Only with multiple, agreed recordings of the same occurrence can truth be found, and even then only in the context of that portion of reality which was recorded. Regardless, it is the work of the credulous to assign value to any recorded fact.

Given the preceding, one might despair that history

---

19 Gustave Le Bon, *The Crowd, A Study of the Popular Mind*

is nothing but the fanciful imaginings of poor observers. In the end this might be true. However, regardless of veracity, such stories as comprise our knowledge of the past are true, inasmuch as they create impression upon the mind and act as a foundation for our present condition. Did Abraham Lincoln indeed walk a mile to return a penny? Did Saint Patrick drive the snakes from Ireland? It does not matter. Regardless of any available proofs, Odysseus remains the trickster demigod and Julius Caesar's last words were "Et tu, Brute?". Legendary heroes, and not real heroes, have built the foundations of modern civilization. Even legends, however, have no stability. The collective mind continually transforms them to suit its needs.

Regardless of whether the collective emotions raised by images are good or bad, they will be both very simple and very exaggerated. Without the fine distinction of reason, the collective mind sees things as a whole and is blind to their development. This exaggeration of sentiments is distilled by suggestion and contagion, which significantly increases its force. The collective goes at once to extremes, because all collective emotion is extreme. A leader is not pleasantly regarded; he is a Godlike presence. A potential enemy is not simply judged with suspicion; he is a devil. Ignorance and envy are released within the collective, as are worship and lust. Where normally public shame or punishment would curb any desire to act on these emotions, the anonymity of the collective removes those obstacles.

The collective is capable of heroism and devotion and soaring virtue, as has been stated previously—more so than in the isolated individual. Given to exaggeration of emotion, a collective is impressed by strong sentiment. A leader who wishes to motivate a collective must make use of violent metaphor, must exaggerate, must endlessly repeat, and must not attempt to explain anything regardless of its dubious nature. Anything which is said, if a speaker is well regarded, is true. Enemies will be brutal, and allies well-loved. Statistics will be accepted without question, and conclusions accepted regardless of logic. Likewise, the heroes or leaders of a collective will be exaggerated within the collective imagination.

Collectives are aware of simple and extreme emotion. The opinions, ideas, and beliefs which are given to them by suggestion are accepted or rejected as a whole, and regarded as either absolute truth or absolute lie. Consider religion on this point, among the oldest of accepted collectives. Dogma does not exist to convey moderation; it dictates absolute right and absolute wrong. Taken in the context of a collective mind, such dogma requires immediacy of action, and extreme action must result. To understand dogma, one must understand how it is viewed by the collective.

The accepted truths of a collective, whether they be dogmatic in nature, organizational, or simply the edifices erected by the collective, are sacred. The Old Bailey in London, England is not simply a building but rather a representation of beloved justice. Buckingham Palace is not simply a large dwelling, but rather a connection with the past power and empire that was once Britain. By association, the resident monarch is held in near god-like esteem by the nation, and afforded privileges which would not be afforded to a common individual. It matters little that in such an enlightened monarchy royalty has slight meaning; it is the image of royalty which both inspires awe and demands loyalty. Without nobility, the societal structure of England would dissolve. As survival is the most pressing need of a collective, English society as it exists today will always demand its nobility.

Dogma is central to the collective, where such organization exists. The dogma must be accepted as a whole, for rejection in part requires self-doubt on the part of the collective. As collectives lack the capacity of reason for self-doubt, such is not possible. This is the case with beliefs which are presented as suggestion rather than by the course of solitary reason. Being unable to discern between truth and error, and having on the other hand a clear understanding of its own strength, the collective is as apt to enforce its own dogma as it is to be intolerant of others. While an individual might be willing to discuss contradictions, the collective will not. Contradictions to accepted dogma on the part of a leader will result in fury from the collective, often to the same degree as the leader's previous accepted divinity.

The inviolability of dogma is found in all collectives, at varying levels of intensity depending upon its parent collective. Sectarian societies give rise to authoritarian and intolerant collectives, while individualistic societies tend to give rise to more tolerant collectives. In the latter case, the term 'tolerant' is relative; all collectives are intolerant.

These notions of authoritarianism and intolerance exist within collectives because they are easily understood and implemented. Reason is not required to demand submission, nor is it necessary to bend another to one's will. These attributes are then well suited to the collective mind, which does not reason yet holds great strength. Likewise, with a clear understanding of their strength, collectives maintain some respect for force and none for kindness, which they regard as weakness. They do not follow easy, forgiving masters, but rather give support to oppressive control. While it is true that Libya's Colonel Qaddafi was both oppressive and dictatorial to his people, it was after he retreated before the might of NATO and the insurgency that his country rose fully against him. It was not his strength which drove him from power, but rather his sudden vulnerability which gave impetus to his opposition. Once his place was secured among the feeble in the mind of his countrymen, he could be murdered with impunity.

A collective is always ready to revolt against the feeble, and to penitently serve the strong. If the leadership of a collective is intermittent, the collective's always-extreme sentiments will swing wildly between hero-worship and revolt. However, to believe that a collective is inherently revolutionary would be to misunderstand its very nature. It is the tendency towards immediate action which lends credence to this false assumption. Rebellious and destructive tendencies are generally transitory. Collectives lack the necessary communal memory to maintain violent action without outside direction, and are too subject to the nature of their parent collectives to be anything other than conservative in regards to their dogma.

Left to themselves, collectives soon become bored with disorder, and return to their ideals of 'normal'.

It is difficult to understand the uprisings of the early 21st century if one does not take into account the conservative nature of collectives. While a collective dedicated to the overthrow of a particular leader may, given the success of their efforts, throw down the institutions of their society, they will in short order replace these institutions with others of near identical nature but under new titles. The institutions existed not because of the dictatorial nature of their hated leader, but because they were necessary extensions of the character of the collective. Similarly, if the character of the collective has not changed, the overthrown dictator will bear little difference to the newly installed leader. Collectives choose that mode of organization which best suits their needs, and this includes their choice in leadership. Likewise, the respect of the collective for traditions is absolute. The collective mind's conservative nature forbids both novelty and change, either in the nature of its institutions or the social mores which allow it to communicate.

This raises the discussion of the possibilities of morality within collectives. If 'morality' is taken to mean repression of instinctual impulse and selfishness, then it is easily seen that the collective mind lacks the conscious control to be moral in any real way. However, if the term morality is taken to mean the short-lived examples of self-sacrifice, devotion, and the desire for perceived justice, then collectives may exhibit at times a high moral character.

Collectives are often shockingly immoral in nature. This is because the savage, destructive instincts which are the inheritance of our savage, destructive past are left dormant in all of mankind. While it is dangerous for the individual to gratify those instincts, within the collective there is no concept of repercussion and the instincts may be followed with impunity. A collective which tortures and kills a single defenseless victim displays cowardice when viewed from a values-based perspective, but it is similar in nature to the pleasure a group of huntsmen might take in the stalking of a deer. A collective might commit murder, arson, theft and rape, but it is also capable of devotion and sacrifice given the correct stimuli. Collectives respond well to calls to patriotism, glory, and honor, often at the cost of their collective lives. How often have collectives offered their lives for ideas and phrases that they scarcely understood?

By way of example, consider the 2006 youth protests of France. These protests were generated in response to the bill entitled "Loi pour l'égalité des chances" or the Equal Opportunity Law. Central to the protests was wording which made it easier for employers to fire employees under the age of 26. The proposed legislation intended to increase competitiveness between France and its international trade partners, as spurred by high unemployment among youth within the country. Understandably, youth protests erupted throughout the nation. What is most interesting about the protests is not the manner in which they proceeded, but that at its outset the country was evenly split on the subject of the bill. Throughout the protest, popular opinion shifted until support for the protesters approached 70%. The facts of the conflict had not changed, but rather the image of discontent was applied to the legislation. Protests grew in size and in popularity not because of reason but because a collective disgust at disorder contributed to the anarchy. One should also note that the majority of the protesters took part not because of outrage over what they had read in the proposed legislation, but rather because of what they had been told by their peers. Factual knowledge of issues is rarely necessary to incite protest.

Personal interest is rarely a powerful motive force within the collective, while it is most often the driving force of the individual. Certainly it was not self-interest which led American volunteers to wars in the closing years of the 20th century which, when viewed rationally and individually, would be incomprehensible. During the Egyptian uprising of what would later be called the Arab Spring, ordinary citizens stood guard against any possible looting of national treasures—treasures they could have easily stolen without notice[20].

If one observes that the collective mind is ruled by unconscious and instinctual motivation, that it is driven to acts of barbarism and selfishness, one must concede that it also sets the example of high morality. If selflessness, stalwart immovability, and absolute devotion to an ideal are moral virtues, then collectives posses these virtues to a

_____

20 "Before the army arrived, young Egyptians — some armed with truncheons grabbed off the police — created a human chain at the museum's front gate to prevent looters from making off with any of its priceless artifacts." from thestar.com, "Citizens help thwart looking (sic) of antiquities", published Jan 30, 2011

higher degree than all but the most vaunted of individuals. It is of no import that the virtues are practiced unconsciously. It is the very incapacity for reason which allows the collective to display these same virtues, and if the collective mind were capable of self-doubt, reason, or self-control, or validity of memory, no doubt civilization on earth might not have risen. If it had by coincidence risen regardless, we would be poorer for the loss of the richness of our illusions. As images and illusions are the foundations for both collective thought and national soul, it is appropriate to examine both of these aspects in greater detail.

Chapter V: The Collective Intellect and Soul

"A nation's culture resides in the hearts and in the soul of its people." – **Mohandas Gandhi**

A study of the development of nations reveals the progression of collectives from disorganization to organization under the effect of all-encompassing ideals. Whether the ideal is the preeminence of Allah, the equality of all men, or divine right is immaterial; the ideal embraces and is embraced by the collective and allows it to focus its ephemeral attention on a single guiding purpose. When these ideals are called into question, the conservatism of the collective reacts strongly and often violently to the assault. If the ideals are removed, there is no focus for the collective and it returns to a disorganized state, often violently angry at the loss of structure, until an acceptable replacement is installed.

Such ideas are simple, and therefore accessible to the collective mind, and as such they may be divided into two classes. The first classification is transitory ideas, the accidental and passing concepts created by the suggestions of the moment: infatuation for a doctrine or individual, for instance. The second classification is fundamental ideas, which hold for the collective great stability—simple yet profound concepts which give rise to still more profound ideas and images, which taken as a whole represent the influences of the parent collective. While transitory ideas are like waves which pass across an ocean and leave little evidence of their passage, fundamental ideas are the ocean itself.

Over the past many decades we see how the waves of transitory ideas may erode the shorelines of the greater, more fundamental ideas which bind together nations. At first observation, it appears that the waves of chance threaten the solidity of national ideal, yet such observation is false. If the shoreline changes,the general shape of its borders remain the same. If waters intrude or retreat from an area, the ocean remains. It represents the sum total of human experience, and is increased by the liters of experience which are the collective intellect and collective soul.

Whether transitory or fundamental in nature, ideas can only affect the collective mind if they are absolute, uncompromising, and simple in shape. They must present themselves in the guise of images, and are only accessible to the collective under this form. While the image of 'Uncle Sam' might seem arbitrary in nature, it grew to iconic stature and came to represent the spirit of self-sacrifice which drove America's efforts in WWII. As the idea the image represented was fundamental in scope, the image remains a part of the American collective soul, a representation which is still used to evoke the ideal of volunteerism.

A transitory idea must present itself in the form of

images, such as 'fat cats' or 'dirty hippies'. Such phrases evoke mental images which are not connected by any logical bond or succession, and may swap places with each other in the collective mind like pages in a flip book[21]. This explains how it is that contradictory ideas can exist side by side in the collective mind. The collective will randomly call to the fore those ideas which are accessible within its intellect based on the requirements of the moment. Ideas translate quickly to action by the processes already shown earlier in this text, and so the collective can seem disingenuous as it shifts between hypocritical actions. The disingenuousness is as much an illusion as the illusion of motion in a flip book. The collective is devoted to the ideal of the moment; it simply has no capacity for self doubt and and little capacity for collective memory. The complete lack of critical nature cannot allow the perception of contradiction.

How is it that the socialist can rail against the excesses of rich capitalists while simultaneously holding in godlike awe the richest and most excessive of socialistic leadership? How is it that the most fervent of the supporters of abortion can angrily oppose capital punishment? How could defenders of individual liberty support such dictatorial concepts such as America's TSA or the Patriot Act? If memory, self-doubt, or critical thinking were present, the answer would be "they cannot." However, without these capacities, each position makes perfect sense. To the conservative mind, it is the duty of a governing body

---

21 Flip books were an early form of animation, in which progressively altered drawings were placed on successive pages. When the pages were turned, the illusion of motion was generated.

to provide for the welfare and protection of its constituents (a concept central to the nature of collectives), and without the concept of dichotomy cannot comprehend that such transitory ideas as The Patriot Act fly in the face of "One nation, under God, with liberty and justice for all."

For an idea to be popularly accessible to the collective mind, it often must undergo drastic transformation. Especially when dealing with complex philosophical or scientific ideas, the modifications necessary for digestion often reduce the parent idea to such a degree that it is unrecognizable. These modifications are dependent on the nature of the collective, or of its parent collective, but the tendency is necessarily towards patronization and simplification. This explains why ideas can be classified so simply when offered in relation to collectives: their simple nature requires no greater division. No matter how laudable an idea might be at its inception, the transformation necessary to provide accessibility to the collective reduces its intellectual value to near nothing.

Because of this, the intellectual value of an idea is without importance. The Christian ideas of the Middle Ages (rule by divine right), the democratic ideas of the Age of Reason (one man, one vote), or the social ideas of the 1970's (I'm OK, You're OK) are not elevated in scope. Their power has been and continues to be immense, however, and they represent the foundations upon which large organized collectives direct themselves.

Even when an idea has transformed to the degree that it is popularly accessible to the collective mind, it cannot exert influence until it has entered the psyche by repetition. This is the work of years, if not decades. Proof of the value of an idea is not enough to raise it to the status of 'truth' in the collective mind. This can be seen by noting how senseless argument is with an individual within a collective. Argument may be offered, backed by the most immutable of proofs, and the individual may (if the argument is of sufficient skill) find himself nodding in eventual agreement. However, upon return to the collective the individual will be seen almost immediately to return to his original stance on the subject of discussion. If the argument were renewed after a period of a few days, it would have to be repeated, again, with fresh logic, and would likewise lack lasting effectiveness. This is the *Law of Mental Unity* at work. To truly alter the individual's position, he must be removed from the collective and placed within a different collective which shares the same sentiments. Once the individual identifies himself with the new collective, then through quick contagion and suggestion the Law of Mental Unity will convert him without further need for argument. To modify popular parlance, you can give a horse water but you can't make it drink; surround it with water, however, and it will drink its fill.

As an example, smokers and non-smokers may be considered collectives unto themselves. A non-smoker may endlessly argue the costs to one's health as a result of smoking, and depending on his skill at argument may eventually gain grudging agreement. The smoker may even agree to quit smoking, and begin upon that path. However, once surrounded by others of like habit, the smoker quickly returns to his old habits, to the mental unity of his smoking collective. If instead the smoker were removed from his collective, from the old haunts around which others of like habits congregate, and were instead welcomed by happy non-smokers, the conversion would quickly take place. It is because of this, and because of the immediacy and the strength of sentiment within a collective, that former smokers seem hypocritically vehement in their opposition to the practice. It is not hypocrisy, but a collective mind which provides the depth and anger of resolve.

When by transformation and repetition an idea has penetrated the collective mind, it possesses an irresistible power and brings about irresistible effects. The ideas which brought about the American revolution were not born in America, but were planted and grown in the minds of philosophers throughout Europe and across the previous century. Their irresistible force is now a matter of historical legend. The concepts of social equality and liberty spread by contagion through the collective European mind until the revered monarchies of the previous epoch were all but eradicated.

A long time is necessary for high concepts to establish themselves in the collective intellect, but just as long a time in necessary for them to be eradicated. Likewise, transitory ideas such as fashion require little time to manifest, and therefore little time to be swept aside. For this reason the collective mind is almost always generations behind the great philosophers whom their leaders might study. Politicians should be well aware of the capacity for error in the understanding of lofty ideals. They must be repeatedly sown within a constituency over a period of years before they will finally take root, and even so will only be properly harvested by later generations.

It should be noted that great ideas are not the only nor the most effective mode of directing a collective. They are but one method, which by virtue of its slow progress allows for modification and adaptation so that they might be implemented in the wisest manner possible. Other methods may be used to much greater effect and slighter time frame, but their effects are necessarily unpredictable and dangerous.

A collective does not reason, nor can it be reasoned with; attempts to do so are doomed to failure. The collective mind does have a process of thought, however it is susceptible to arguments which are logically so basic that they may only be considered analogy. The reasoning of the collective intellect, as with the reasoning of the individual intellect, is based upon the association of ideas. Within the collective intellect, however, this association is only through analogy or succession. The reasoning might be considered magical thinking, in nature; it is akin to the primitive belief that devouring the heart of a foe confers their strength to the victor, or that of a worker who believes all employers are exploitative because of his poor experience with a single employer.

The reasoning of the collective intelligence consists of the power of association of unlike things which hold only thread bare connection, and broad generalization; arguments of this kind should be offered to collectives if they are to be influenced. A logical argument might report well to the individual mind, but will be incomprehensible to the collective. One might be astonished at the weakness of speeches which are delivered to different collectives, then further astonished at the enormous influence they had on the collective mind. The speeches were intended to convince collectives, and not individuals. Logic was not necessary—only the presentation of acceptable images which, when taken in succession, created a chain of reasoning which might be grasped by the collective intellect.

The suggestibility of the collective mind and its primitive form of reason prevents it from utilizing any form of critical spirit which does not abide by the *Law of Mental Unity*. That is, the collective mind is incapable of discerning truth from error beyond those great truths which have already integrated themselves into the collective soul, nor is the collective able to form any sort of judgment on any matter. Judgments which are accepted by collective minds are those value assessments which are forced upon them by their leadership, and not those which are adopted after contemplation. The ease at which they gain general acceptance is a result of the impossibility of the collective mind to form an opinion unique to itself and based on its own reasoning.

To fully understand the reasoning methods of the collective, it is now necessary to introduce a new concept: *The Principle of Inversion*: *for any given collective at any given time, abstract concepts will tend to achieve the status of concrete objects while concrete objects will tend to devolve to the status of abstraction.*

Consider, as an example, the Christian collective (as opposed to the doctrines of the church, which may differ). Within Christianity, worship is given to a God who neither reveals himself to his followers nor allows idols of himself to be manufactured. The veracity of his existence is moot, in this consideration. The concept of God is an abstraction which is treated as a concrete reality by the collective. In relation, God commands His people to give freely of themselves. If goods and services are devoted to the work of God, He rewards His faithful. The concrete cost of such goods and services is treated as an abstraction, even though their concrete nature is easily seen.

Consider, as a second example, a large protest of students in any given city. The concepts and principles upon which the protest is based will be spoken of as concrete objects or individuals. Phrases such as, "We want to bring democracy to our society!" reflect not just a desire for change, but also a notion that a political system is a concrete object which might be passed physically from one individual to another. At the same time, the protesters will freely give among themselves supplies and commodities as if they were without cost. Armed forces set against them will be nothing more than ideas which may be pushed aside. Even given the feeling of overwhelming strength, how is it that a single protester in Tienanmen square detained an entire column of armed tanks unless the protester himself had some sense of the unreality of their existence? When such unreality is shattered, the collective will react angrily and often violently to the dissolution of their misconceptions. How dare a truck overrun a pedestrian who jumped into its path? The result of the action might be perfectly understandable and predictable, but the imposition of the concrete upon the abstract could only yield further anger and opposition.

Given the Principle of Inversion, the subject of the collective imagination gains particular importance. The figurative imagination of collectives is very powerful, very active, and very susceptible to impression. The images evoked in the collective mind by a person, an event, or an accident are as concrete as reality. Collectives operate within a dream, wherein their limited reason allows images of extreme intensity which would just as quickly disappear from the mind if they could be subjected to the non-existent influences of self doubt or contemplation. As the collective mind has no self-doubt or capacity for contemplation, the improbable does not exist. It should be noted that the most improbable of occurrences have the greatest impact on the imagination.

Does the collective have a soul? If one accepts that the word 'soul' refers to that sense of personality which differentiates one individual from another, then the answer is 'yes.' Collectives may differ from each other in myriad ways, based almost entirely upon the nature of the images in which they think and the abstractions they treat as concrete. If one defined 'soul' as that quality which allows the creation of art or literature, or which defines beauty and good and evil, then the answer is 'yes.' Collectives, through use of their unique dogma, have a very clear understanding of those qualities which may be termed 'good' or 'evil' or 'beautiful', and as a result their constituent individuals may create great works by virtue of their membership within the collective. Finally, if one accepts that a 'soul' is that incomprehensible quality of a living being which allows it to continue its existence even beyond death and utter destruction, then the answer is 'yes.'

Collectives manifest a quality upon their constituents which may be categorized as the *Principle of Imprint*:

> *Once an individual has been accepted within the collective mind and become subject to the Law of Mental Unity, the images and ideas with which he thinks will forever be changed. These images and ideas may be reduced in emotional value, or altered with the addition of new images and ideas, but never erased.*

This quality ensures that, even if a collective is irrevocably disbanded, it will continue to influence its surroundings by virtue of the effect its members have on subsequent collectives.

Many centuries have passed since the death of both Alexander the Great and his empire, yet the influence of this collective continues to ensure that men shave their faces in much of the civilized world (an affectation which, up to that point, was rarely seen among men). More recently, yet still thousands of years into the past, Rome passed irrevocably into the annals of failed nations. Yet its influence upon modern society continues even today. The theatrical plays of Greece continue to provide ample fodder for theaters, and the adaptation of their plots continue to be source material for modern playwrights. Centuries after the death of Eleanor of Aquitaine, her 'court of love' continues to influence the mating rituals of a huge percentage of mankind. The images of collective imagination, once entered into the racial memory, do not fade. They endure, they are passed from parent to child, and their influence is continued in perpetuity.

The marvelous and legendary are the true supports of any long-lived collective. Appearances play a much more important part than reality in the history of collectives, where through the *Principle of Inversion* the unreal is of greater import than the real. Collectives are only capable of thinking in images, and are only impressed by images. It is only images which terrify them, and it is only images which attract them. To this end, to motivate collectives to action, only images will suffice.

For this reason, movies, television, and theater, in which the images are seemingly made concrete, have the capacity for great motivating effect upon the collective. The airing of single movie entitled *The Day After*[22], had such a profound affect upon the United States that almost only by the virtue of its presentation the United States and United Soviet Socialist Republic grudgingly resumed the process of

---

22 *The Day After, 1983;* ABC Circle Films, Writer: Edward Humes, Director: Nicholas Meyer

treaties which ended with a world-wide ban on nuclear proliferation. The remarkable nature of this singular work of fiction is understandable when one understands the reasons for the power of dramatic literature and theater.

Throughout the ages, this effect has not varied. The entire audience simultaneously experiences the same emotions, and if these emotions are not at once transformed into acts, it is because no member of the audience can deny that the show is the result of illusion, and he has laughed or cried over the imaginary. Through the *Principle of Inversion*, the unreal has become real, and is treated as though real by the individual intellect so long as the viewer remains with the collective audience. At the show's end and upon leaving the theater, the individual leaves the collective audience and recognizes the falsity of the show. Yet through the *Principle of Imprint*, the images remain a permanent part of his psyche, ready to influence his actions and the intellect of any collectives of which he might be a member. Great historical collective movements, through the rise of Buddhism, the spread of Christianity, and the growth of Islam, the Reformation, the French Revolution, and the rise and fall of Communism, have been the direct or indirect result of impressions produced upon the collective imagination.

Furthermore, history's most effective leaders have, whether by design or instinct, governed not in opposition to the collective imagination but in coordination with it. Without propaganda, it is unlikely that Hitler could have risen to power or Stalin retained it. To this end, leaders should understand that the most effective methods of motivating the collective is through the window of their imagination.

Whatever strikes the collective imagination presents itself as a very clear image, freed from explanation except by virtue of miracles, great hope, or great victory, great crime, or the like. Abstractions must be presented to the collective imagination as a whole, without explanation of how they came to exist. A hundred crimes or accidents will not affect the collective imagination so much as the death of a single child, a single victim of wasting illness, or a single horrific accident. The reason for this is that the collective imagination can easily call up the image of the dead child, or the dying man, or the twisted automobile. The collective mind is incapable, however, of calling up an image of a thousand dead men. Two images captured the collective imagination of the United States on September 11, 2001 and provided the impetus for the reformation of the collective will: an airplane crashing into the World Trade Center[23], and a victim leaping to his death from its roof rather than suffer death by inferno[24]. Following the disaster, President George W. Bush presented an image which forever linked him to the disaster as a strong and compassionate leader. On the site of what later became known as 'Ground Zero'[25] he stood atop a platform with his arm around a fireman and spoke to the assembled crowd of rescue workers (and

---

23 September 11, 2001, as shown on multiple news networks

24 Also September 11, 2001, later in the day.

25 This term has been discouraged by the New York City Government, in favor of "The World Trade Center and the National September 11th Memorial and Museum." The new moniker lacks the imagery of the original name, and so is not widely used.

by virtue of television, the world) through a bull-horn.[26] Ten years later, few can recall the content of his speech, but all can remember this iconic image, and the phrase, "But I can hear you, and soon the whole world is going to hear you!"

It is not reason which will move a collective, but imagery. It is not historical fact, but the way it took place which maintains the highest importance. To have impact upon the collective imagination and currency within the collective mind, concepts and directives should be tied to a striking image. To understand such imagery and its effect on the collective mind is to understand the principles behind a common characteristic which helps to give lasting cohesion to nearly every collective: the cult of the collective.

---

26 September 14, 2001, as distributed through several channels of media.

Chapter VI: The Cult of the Collective

"It is a truism that almost any sect, cult, or religion will legislate its creed into law if it acquires the political power to do so." – **Robert A. Heinlein**

The collective mind has very little capacity for reason. It accepts or rejects ideas as a whole, and tolerates neither discussion nor contradiction. The suggestions brought to bear on it invade the entire field of its understanding and tend to create the need for immediate action. Once influenced, the collective will is ready to sacrifice its members in pursuit of an ideal or overarching concept with which it has been inspired. The collective is only capable of violent or extreme emotion; sympathy becomes love, jealousy becomes hatred, and principle becomes martyrdom.

These general qualities aptly describe the general characteristics common to collectives. When they are examined as they relate to times of political upheaval or religious fervor, they conform to a nature which could best be described as the *Cult of the Collective*.

> *The Cult of the Collective is the capacity for a collective, when influenced by a charismatic ideal*

or leader, to achieve religious fervor. While not all collectives achieve cult status, all cults are collectives.

It is important to note that the word 'cult', as used here, is used without value assessment or other connotation. Likewise no value assessment is made of any collectives which are used for examples or analogies. Study of collectives requires that this great effort be made, so that fatal errors may be avoided. Too often assessments as to the value of religious sentiments have resulted in war, mass murder, and generational antipathy. Cold-blooded rationalism in regard to collectives will avoid this pitfall.

As the overall nature of a collective is necessarily simple, so too is the nature of the *Cult of the Collective.* Its characteristics may include worship of a supposedly superior being who represents an ideal, fear of the being's supposed power, and blind submission to its commands, capacity and/or willingness to discuss its dogmas only by rote, and the desire to spread the dogmas regardless of comprehension, and a tendency to consider as enemies any who do not accept such dogmas. Whether the cult applies to one or more gods, to a wooden or stone idol, or to a hero or a political concept, so long as it exhibits the given characteristics, it in essence will always remain a cult.

Belief in the supernatural and miraculous will usually be present as well. The *Cult of the Collective* equates a mysterious power to the ideal or hero to which it devotes its enthusiasm. The individual who worships a deity is not necessarily part of the collective cult. This characteristic occurs when he devotes the greater part of his mental resources to the worship of a cause or personality, willingly submits his will to the same, and delivers fanaticism at the service of that cause or personality which becomes both goal and guide of his thoughts and actions.

Intolerance and fanaticism are necessary for elements within the collective to become the *Cult of the Collective*. They are the inevitable result of those who believe themselves to possess secret knowledge. These two characteristics are found in collectives when they are inspired by a great conviction of any kind. White Supremacists could be considered a collective cult, as could the U.S. Marine Corps or the Tea Party. Business corporations normally have the *Cult of the Collective* at their core[27], and non-profit corporations often rise to this level of ardor[28]. Leaders who have inspired followings of this nature include Vladamir Lenin, General Douglas MacArthur, and Chairman Mao Tse-Tung.

Collectives in general maintain the overall characteristics of submission, intolerance, and the need for propaganda. One might well remark that all collective ideals have a religious form. The hero acclaimed by a crowd is a veritable god for that collective, at least for the moment. For a short time after the attacks of September 11, 2001, President George W. Bush exhibited much this level

---

[27] A fine example of this is the former internet company Mindspring, which under the leadership of CEO Charles Brewer generated a cult-like following in its employees. Other less striking examples may be found in the legions of 'workaholics' who maintain the culture within other corporations such as FedEx, BP, and IBM.

[28] Greenpeace and Code Pink are both excellent examples in this category.

of esteem among his supporters. Founders of religious or political creeds have spread them solely because they were successful in inspiring collectives with fanatical sentiments which convinced them to lay down their lives in support of the ideal.

The empire of Rome dominated history for 500 years. This has been often enough remarked by historians that it requires no further discussion here. It is of note that during that time, thirty legions commanded a hundred million to obedience. This would not have been possible without the *Cult of the Collective:* in this case the worship of Caesar. While altars and churches are no longer erected to great men, they do have statues, and their admirers carry their portraits. The cult of which they are the object is not far distant from that of Rome. When the collective requires a god, it will elevate one before anything else. These are not merely superstitions which may be opposed with reason. The collective cult represents a manifestation of the collective mind, and is therefore immune to reason (and indeed may violently strike against such attempts).

It is therefore not necessary for the collective that they have a religion, because where necessary a collective will create those deities it requires. Even atheism, at its core, exhibits the intolerance of a religious sentiment. Quoting Le Bon:

> *"The great historian Taine has only studied the Revolution as a naturalist, and on this account the real genesis of events has often escaped him. He has perfectly observed the facts, but from want of*

having studied the psychology of crowds he has not always been able to trace their causes. The facts having appalled him by their bloodthirsty, anarchic, and ferocious side, he has scarcely seen in the heroes of the great drama anything more than a horde of epileptic savages abandoning themselves without restraint to their instincts. The violence of the Revolution, its massacres, its need of propaganda, its declarations of war upon all things, are only to be properly explained by reflecting that the Revolution was merely the establishment of a new religious belief in the mind of the masses."[29]

The great heroes and great villains of history, then, cannot be solely the leaders who are selected by collectives for admiration. While these leaders undoubtedly had great effect over the movement of such collectives, they were in the end supported because they represented such sentiments as their collectives required. The millions who suffered planned starvation at the hands of the People's Republic of China were not the victims of Mao Tse-Tung, per se, but of the communal mind of the people themselves. While Adolf Hitler led the destruction of the Jewish people within his growing Third Reich, the destruction was the result of a collective mind which submitted itself to the figure it had promoted to godhood. Again, quoting Le Bon:

"The most absolute power of the most despotic monarch can scarcely do more than hasten or retard the moment of their apparition. the

---

29 Gustave Le Bon, *The Crowd, A Study of the Popular Mind*

massacre of Saint Bartholomew or the religious wars were no more the work of kings than the Reign of Terror was the work of Robespierre, Danton, or Saint Just. At the bottom of such events is always to be found the working of the soul of the masses, and never the power of potentates."[30]

---

30 Ibid.

Chapter VII: The Origins of the Ideologies of Collectives

"Great ideology creates great times." – **Kim Jong Il**

Having reached an understanding as to the underlying mental state of any given collective, and also as to the underlying feelings, intellect, and reasoning power, it is appropriate to understand how opinions and beliefs arise within collectives and become established. Two factors contribute to such intellectual property: remote factors and immediate factors. The remote factors allow crowds to adopt certain convictions and completely reject others. Such factors are analogous to the tilling of a field within which new crops may grow. Without an understanding of farming methods, the appearance of crops might well seem magical in nature. Similarly, the sudden appearance of striking ideologies might seem miraculous. The practice of preparing a population for the planting of ideas is a generational pursuit, yet when such crops yield their fruit it is usually not just sudden but rather an orgy of awakening.

Immediate factors, after the long preparatory work, serve as the catalyst to bring the new ideas into being. To use the previous analogy, a plot of land may be tilled and fertilized, and seeds planted, to no avail. It is not until the rains come that the seeds germinate and young plants begin to stretch towards the sun. The revolutions which spring unexpectedly from an otherwise content populace spring from these factors. It is due to them that a riot breaks out or a strike is decided upon, and to them that majorities install dictators or replace elected officials.

These two types of factors can be seen in those great historical events which involved collectives. The American revolution did not begin in America but can trace its origins as far back as democratic Athens. Additionally, the colonies had been populated with such individualistic thinkers and educated rebellious persons that monarchical societies could neither tolerate nor kill. With the ground thus tilled and planted, it was the immediate factor of heavy taxation by the British which served as the catalyst to bring the ideas to fruition. As taxation lowered the colonists' perceived comparative status, they identified not with a remote monarch but with each other and a leadership which was more inclined to speak than to remain silent, better suited to capitalism than to state-ownership, and more amicable to self-rule than to servility.

There are many possibilities for remote factors, but the most important are found to most strongly affect the beliefs and opinions of collectives: collective soul, traditions, and time, institutions, and education. Other remote factors might play a part, but these are the most striking.

The collective soul is approached first, because it dwarfs the other remote effects in its power. A collective soul possesses such power that its beliefs, institutions and arts are merely the outward expression of its inner nature. The great nation of Canada sprang fully formed from the womb of Mother England, and although through the working of time its soul has altered somewhat, the nation continues to show the mirrored heredity of nature and civilization. Given identical circumstances, Canada would today be a very different country with a very different nature had it instead sprung from the collective soul of France or Spain or Germany. No idea, regardless of its nature, may pass unchanged from one collective soul to another. English democracy differs from American democracy which in turn differs from Turkish democracy. Even if identifiable forms are used, such as the parliamentary system, the nature of each parliament is different enough that one may see the inevitable effect of the collective soul on the institution. Environment, circumstances, and events represent the social suggestions of the moment. They may have a considerable influence, but such influence is transitory if if it is contrary to the nature of the collective soul--that is, the accumulation of civilization inherited by its ancestral line. This is why collectives of different countries offer considerable differences of beliefs and conduct and may not be influenced in the same manner.

Traditions represent the ideas, the needs, and the collective memories of the past. They are the synthesis of the collective soul, and impose great force on the collective actions. Quoting Le Bon:

> "...many statesmen are still no further advanced

than the theorists of the [18th Century] who believed that a society could break off with its past and be entirely recast on lines suggested solely by the light of reason. A people is an organism created by the past, and, like every other organism, it can only be modified by slow hereditary accumulations."[31]

Traditions guide men, even more so when they are part of an active collective. Those accustomed habits which form the basis of society become more pronounced and important when the conscious mind is subverted and one is thrust into a situation of being surrounded by the unfamiliar. The armed services make good use of this tendency, as conveyed by a common axiom, "when a man is under stress, he reverts to his training." One might stress this as a rule of collectives, but as the collectives are generally not composed of individuals with identical training, such a rule would only suffice in matters of armed services.

The effect of traditions on the collective mind is not necessarily a bad thing. Neither the collective soul nor civilization itself is possible without tradition. Because of this, the two great struggles of mankind since the beginning of civilization have been to first create a network of traditions which enable social prosperity, and then to destroy such traditions when their perceived benefits no longer exceed their perceived cost. Civilization is impossible without tradition, and progress is impossible without the destruction of the same. The difficulty is to find

31 Gustave Le Bon, *The Crowd, A Study of the Popular Mind*

a balance between stability and vitality. If traditions become too firmly rooted, such as in 18th-century China, the collective becomes stagnant and incapable of evolution. In this case violent revolution is of no use, because the society so overthrown will either immediately gather together the vestiges of its traditions and rebuild them anew, or leave them scattered and descend into chaos and annihilation. The history of the Assyrian captivity of the Hebrews is an example of a people who, through tradition alone, rose from virtual destruction to renewed national identity. The ideal, then, is to preserve the traditions of the past yet allow them to change slightly, little by little, as the needs of the collective dictate. This is a condition which has been realized by Rome, England, and more recently the United States. Indeed, one might conclude that the United States has codified change into its national identity.

Collectives cling the most tenaciously to traditional ideas and oppose change with the most obstinacy. This is most notable with collectives categorized as castes, or collectives whose membership is dependent on parentage. Collectives are extremely conservative in nature, regardless of the nature of their ideals, and the most violent of rebellions generally end in altered words and terms. After a long and bloody revolution, following the victory of the Army of George Washington against England, the congress of the United States jubilantly offered to install General Washington as monarch, trading a distant tyrant for one more immediate. Had Washington accepted, history would doubtless have pursued a much different course. Again quoting Le Bon,

"The most redoubtable idols do not dwell in temples, nor the most despotic tyrants in palaces; both the one and the other can be broken in an instant. But the invisible masters that reign in our innermost selves are safe from every effort at revolt, and only yield to the slow wearing away of centuries."[32]

In social equations, as in biological equations, time is one of the most immutable factors. It is the only real creator and the only great destroyer. Time has grown mountains from plains, and brought unicellular life to the point of human dignity. Gustave Le Bon conjectures that *"A being possessed of the magical force of varying time at his will would have the power attributed by believers to God."*

Concerning collectives, however, one need only concern one's self with the effect of time on the creation of ideas and opinions. Its effect in this regard is still powerful. It is integral in the formation of the collective soul, and it causes the germination, birth, and growth, and death of ideals. By virtue of time great thoughts gain both strength and traction, and by this same virtue they wither and die when their value has been erased.

In particular, time allows the sowing of the seeds of opinions and ideas so central to collectives, or at least prepares the ground within which they may germinate. This is why some great ideas have been possible in one age and not in another. Time accumulates, through repeated

---

32 Gustave Le Bon, *The Crowd, A Study of the Popular Mind*

discussion in private rooms, that critical mass of idea and opinion which eventually must either blossom forward as ideal or be abandoned for more effective thought. Ideals are not born at the prime of their volatile adolescence. They must struggle first to crawl, then to stand, and finally to walk before they may run forward into the light of spring and compete among each other. To understand their parentage, one must look into the deep recesses of past. They are the daughters of a barbaric past and the mothers of an unknown future, but always the slaves of time.

Time is therefore the master of the collective, and one need only allow its action to see all things transformed. Quoting Le Bon,

> "*At the present day we are very uneasy with regard to the threatening aspirations of the masses and the destructions and upheavals foreboded thereby. Time, without other aid, will see to the restoration of equilibrium.*"[33]

The concept that institutions can repair the defects of any society, that progress is the consequence of changes in institutions and governments, and that social changes may be affected by the decrees of either a monarch or a bureaucracy is still accepted, even as it was generally accepted in the 19th century. It was the overarching belief behind the great wars of the 20th century and continues to be the genesis of the wars and revolutions of the 21st

---

33 Gustave Le Bon, *The Crowd, A Study of the Popular Mind*

century. That the experience of mankind since he first gathered into the budding nations of pre-history shows otherwise has not sufficed to dissuade the world's leaders.

Institutions are the manifestation of the soul of the collective, and the collective soul cannot be recast by legislative action or royal decree. A collective does not choose its institutions any more than a dog chooses its coloring. Institutions and governments are the product of the ideas, beliefs and customs of a collective, and are built not by the leadership caste to control the collective but by the collective to control itself. They are not the creators of an age, but the product of it. Collectives are governed not by fashion but by tradition, as their character decides they will be governed. Political systems evolve over centuries, and centuries are required to change them. Institutions have no virtue: of themselves they are neither good nor evil. Those which are of value to a given collective will be destructive to another. While *Robert's Rules of Order*[34] may allow structured discussion within a political gathering, one would not expect a drug cartel to abide by them.

It is not in the power of a collective to change its institutions in any meaningful way. At the cost of blood and violence it can change their name, but in their essence they will live on unmodified. Afghanistan, a nation which was initially ruled by a tribal government, received 'enlightenment' from its repeated wars with the superpowers. Although democratic reforms were imposed it remains tribal in nature. If the leaders have changed, or

---

34 *US Army Brig. Gen. Henry Martin Robert* published *Robert's Rules of Order* in 1876, as a guide to parliamentary proceedings. They are widely considered a guide for fair and impartial proceedings to this day.

the laws have been modified for the moment, only a fundamental change in the nature of the people will allow that its institutions will not return to the theocracy of the past. The people of a collective impose, by virtue of their collective mind and soul, institutions which function to control those impulses they feel are detriment to the functioning of society. Only the people of the collective, therefore, can meaningfully change those institutions through self-sacrifice, self-realization, and incremental revolution.

To waste time in the imposition of constitutions on unwilling peoples is therefore a fruitless task. A people will benefit from a constitution only if they have themselves willingly developed the document, and certainly not under the watchful eye of a leadership caste which does not participate in their collective soul. Necessity and time will complete the task of enumerating rights and responsibilities far better than self-appointed saviors, and with far greater effect. The practice of imposition of law upon the unwitting is a much-enjoyed pastime of nations, yet a waste of effort which might be better spent in the slow passage of knowledge and ideas across borders.

To take the laws and dogma of each people and show to what extent they are an expression of the needs of each collective soul would require the work of generations, and therefore is not attempted here. It shall suffice, then, to note that such institutions such as law and dogma are immune to violent upheaval. It is possible, for instance, to rationally discuss the advantages or disadvantages of centralized government. When one observes a nation of very different peoples devote several hundreds of years of effort to attaining this ideal, only to see it overthrown by great revolution and replaced with different centralization, we must grudgingly observe that despite such violent outbursts such centralization is required by the national soul. Such was the case with the French Revolution and the American Civil War. After such revolution, the tendency towards centralization was strengthened. Such is the power of institutions. They are the outcome of collective need, a condition of the continued existence of the nation in question. We should pity the naiveté of politicians who speak of an institution's destruction. If by chance of fate they should succeed, their success would at once be signal for bloodshed on a scale which would shock even the most jaded of imaginations, and would result in the resumption of the institution under a new name.

One must conclude, therefore, that it is not in institutions that influence is to be found upon the soul of the collective. When one sees such countries as the United States reach high prosperity under a democratic republic, while others, such as Greece, flounder and fail under a socialized democracy, we must admit that the institution of democracy is as foreign to the success of one as it is the failure of the other. Collectives are governed by their collective soul, and institutions which are not directly modeled on that character represent nothing more than a borrowed coat, or a mask to hide a scar. No doubt wars will continue to be waged on the pretext of dragging the unwilling to the improper, that they may be blessed by the relics of another nation's saints. Without a shared religion such relics will be no more than the bones and dust of the brave who die for such pointless exercise.

In one sense, institutions may seem to act on the mind of the collective to the point that they engender such upheavals. In reality it is not the institutions that act in this manner. Whether victor or vanquished, they possess in themselves no virtue. It is illusions and words that have influence on the mind of the collective, and especially words—words which are as powerful as they are fleeting.

Education is the doorway to the soul of a collective, and once opened may not easily be shut. It is often considered that this is the only way to affect change to a people and by this action improve them and make them equal. By its constant repetition, this assertion has become one of the most steadfast dogmas of Western thought. It is as difficult to attack it as it is to attack the dogma of the church amongst the faithful. However, any attempt to understand the interaction of collectives must include at least a cursory examination of the effect of their educational system, and this text would be remiss if it did not include such an item here.

The public/private educational system differs from nation to nation and from collective to collective. However, at least one aspect remains constant—the importance of early childhood education within the most basic (and therefore the most integral) collective: the family unit. Children are possessed of a genius almost at birth, if not before, which allows them to learn through direct observation. Initial in their education is the immediate concept that the female is the nurturing concept, the gateway for sustenance and love. The mother provides for their needs, maintains their hygiene, and is initially their source for instruction on social interaction: speech, physical intimacy and self-direction. Secondly, the they learn socially acceptable male-female role interaction from the father. Regardless of the gender of the dominant personality within the family unit, the child learns to follow the strongest leader and to obey. Finally, from siblings and other children of like age, they are given the opportunity to practice such interactions and to learn socially acceptable behavior such as sharing or dominant/submissive behavior. In such cases, the child craves direction and instruction as to what is allowable activity versus activity which results in punishment. The collective mind of the family is imprinted upon the child in what is normally a safe and supportive environment, and this becomes the foundation for other experiences within his or her life. Here they learn that fire burns, that water is either fun or to be feared, and that insects crawl (and sometimes bite), the importance of cleanliness, acceptable language, and often the ability to read and their own self worth. This is the point of growth for society and the pillar upon which it stands.

It is upon reaching the first plateau of growth, that point within the family collective at which the child is considered capable of entering the educational collective, that the child is allowed to develop beyond this basic collective mind and is forced to violate the first learned rule of life: stay with the group. Sometimes traumatic, this lesson of life is integral for the their understanding of inter-collective instability and creates in a very short time an emotional image relating to their place in a very big world. From this point forward until the child completes their education, the learning which was at first the sole province of the family collective is gradually transitioned until nearly all learning is provided by a central authority. That authority becomes the dominant personality in the child's life until such time as he or she leaves the educational collective and enters society as a whole, to socially interact as they have been taught, develop intimate relationships as they have been taught, and to reproduce as they have been taught, and to take such a place within a newly created family collective as they have been taught. In this manner, the continuance of both a family soul and a larger national collective pursues its circular track and the solidity of the foundations of society is assured.

Why should these principles be mentioned here if they are so basic? If one understands how to build a thing, then one understands how it may be likewise destroyed. If any of these basic preliminary concepts are removed or subverted on a wholesale basis, then the entirety of the larger collective is likewise changed for better or worse, and without remedy. Hitler understood this when, as one of his first grand actions in the building of the master race, he completely reworked the educational system. Likewise, figures such as Mussolini, Mao-Tse-Tung, and Rockefeller, and Saddam Hussein utilized the educational system to solidify their positions as the predominant personality within their respective societies.

If one were to remove even one of the basic supports

of the family collectives, what would happen? Initially, the family collective would instinctively fill the void with their own membership. If the mother figure was removed, then either the father or the child would attempt to fill the position. Failing this, the father as dominant personality would attempt to find a replacement mother figure—a grandmother or aunt or an individual from a completely different family collective. Each time the mother position was changed, the family's collective mind would change and new impression would be created within the mind of the child. If no replacement were possible and the father was unable or unwilling to fill the mother-figure position, then the child would either have to adapt by permanently becoming the mother figure or a centralized authority would have to be utilized. With this eventuality, the centralized authority would gain in stature in the mind of the child to become a representation of love, discipline, and sustenance, leading to sentiments which would alter his views throughout the rest of his life. Such division of labor is both instinctual and necessary, so one or several of these remedies must be utilized, to the detriment of the whole.

In what may be seen as a subordinate collective growing and overcoming a larger, parent collective, an educational system may be used to significantly alter the collective character, intellect, and eventually the soul. Centralized education allows affected children to be taught the same image-set (or collective thoughts) and control of that image-set is mental control of the most powerful order. More importantly, eventually the centralized educational system will grow with the population to such a point that it forms a collective mind of its own. In such a case the educational collective claims near-religious possession of knowledge and reason, and conveys such belief to the children under its charge. A collective is a living being, and exhibits the classic driving motivations inherent to the nature of living creatures. It feeds on individual membership, and expels waste products in the form of individuals who cannot or will not conform to the collective will. It reproduces itself through the spread of concepts and ideas, in a form of social mitosis. Most importantly, it must survive and will undertake any action within its power, within the bounds of its own moral restrictions, to ensure that survival. Educational collectives are no different, in this sense, than other collectives. As they are composed of individuals who do not share identical training, discipline, or specialty, they will act not as organized collectives (that is, a collectives dedicated to a single narrow purpose) but as disorganized collectives (that is, collectives of dissimilar individuals). To direct such entrenched collective minds requires not the distant factors as were just discussed, but immediate factors which may direct their progress, shape their actions, and trigger ideas in the desired manner.

Chapter VIII: Immediate Factors on Collective Opinion

"Reality is merely an illusion, albeit a very persistent one." – **Albert Einstein**

As an understanding has been reached in how remote factors provide fertile ground for the implantation of ideas, it is appropriate now to discuss those immediate factors which may sway the collective mind either to action or inaction, depending on their nature. Given comprehension of the basic laws and principles of collectives, one may already hold a basic understanding of the methods with which they may be affected, through use of ideas, contagion, and, importantly, suggestion. As suggestions are constantly available to any collective mind, such a mind is naturally resistant to all but the most directly affecting information. Additionally, the factors which affect the collective may differ significantly depending on the underlying structure and parent collective from which it rose. Gustave Le Bon compares collectives to the Sphinx of ancient Greek myth: *"it is necessary to arrive at a solution of the problems... or to resign ourselves to being devoured by them."*[35]

---

35 Gustave Le Bon, *The Crowd, A Study of the Popular Mind*

When studying the collective imagination, one finds that it is open to those impressions produced by images. The images need not be physical; it is possible to evoke them through use of effective words and formulas. If skillfully used, speech possesses a mystical quality. It can cause within the collective mind an all-encompassing storm, or calm the same as if with a wave of the hand. One could likely bridge the ocean of their choice with the bodies of those who have martyred themselves for little more than the skillful words of a trusted leader.

The power of words is bound up with the images they bring to mind, and is independent of their real definition. Quite often the most ill-defined words evoke the strongest images. Examples might be "democracy", "socialism", or "freedom", "liberalism", or "conservatism", "human-rights", or "civil-liberties". To understand any of these terms it is necessary to be well-read on the subject which they label, yet nearly any member of society can recite them and bring to mind an image which they evoke. Likewise, such images vary between collectives. Mystical power is attached to those words, as if their understanding might yield eternal happiness. They represent dreams, and the hope of their fulfillment.

Reasoned argument is incapable of combating certain words. They are spoken in hushed tones and treated with solemn respect in the presence of collectives, and as soon as they have been pronounced the respect for their abstract meaning is palpable. Many may consider their underlying nature to be a natural force or supernatural power. The images they evoke are vague, yet grandiose—it is this vagueness which makes them obscure and powerful. In societies which have cast aside the governing force of religion, they represent new gods to which men may bow as willing servants. As their concrete definition differs from their abstract meaning, they vary between collectives even if the collectives share the same language. A word as simple as 'profit' evokes very different meanings between liberal and conservative minds. Transitory images are attached to the words, then, and the word is simply a gate through which such images may pass into the collective conscious.

All speech does not contain the power of imagery. Used without skill, speech may very well reduce such words to nothing more than meaningless sound, unable to evoke response of any kind, and whose only use is as a form of linguistic shorthand. Quoting Le Bon, "*Armed with a small stock of formulas and commonplaces learnt while we are young, we possess all that is needed to traverse life without the tiring necessity of having to reflect on anything whatever.*"[36]

Consider the word 'liberty' as an excellent example. The meaning of 'liberty' today might represent the capacity to choose one's favorite restaurant, or travel where one wishes, or to simply avoid participation in any social activity whatsoever. How could an individual born in the mid-1990's comprehend the reverence once held for such a word at a time when liberty of thought was a luxury afforded solely to aristocracy? Could any citizen of Western Society truly understand the degree of fear held by citizens

---

36 Gustave Le Bon, *The Crowd, A Study of the Popular Mind*

of the 1600's when faced with the prospect of discussion of religion, science, or government? If a word such as 'liberty' might change in abstract meaning to this degree, how much more difficult might be more complex concepts?

Speech, then, has only passing significance, which changes from year to year and between collectives. If one wishes to affect a collective, both speaker and listener must have identical definitions for the terms which are used. Without such unanimity of definition such speech is fruitless at best, and disastrous at worst. By way of explanation, one might recall the well-meant phrase 'happy campers' as used by Vice President Dan Quayle when addressing a collection of American Samoans[37], or the joking use of president Jimmy Carter of the phrase 'Montezuma's Revenge'[38] to a gathering of Mexican citizens. Both phrases evoked different images dependent upon the nations in which they were delivered.

Therefore, when a collective has come to have extreme hatred for the images associated with certain words, the first duty of a speaker is to change the words without varying the things to which the words refer. 'Madman' must become 'Terrorist', then 'Radical'. The object of the descriptive word remains untouched. Only the label is changed, and the speaker hopes to have therefore in some way changed the underlying abstract definition. When a collective cannot endure the images raised by a concept, the concept's abstract definition must be changed —otherwise discussion must cease. As communication is

---

37 Speech to American Samoans, April, 1989
38 February, 1979, at a luncheon honoring the President in Mexico City

the lifeblood of a collective, cessation is not a viable option.

Such is this power of words that it can transform the very nature of an institution by virtue of a new label. A regime may lend validity to its dictatorial rule by labeling itself democratic, regardless of the existence of any valid electoral process. The art of effective government is comprised of the study of effective speech. One of the greatest difficulties of this study is that in the same society the same words may often have very different meanings for different classes of individual. In such cases, what was previously mentioned becomes evident; changes in abstract short-hand easily render definitions useless between collectives.

Every civilization requires its illusions. The creators of illusions have, throughout history, inspired more temples, statues, and alters than to any other class of men. Whether it is the religious illusions of Moloch and Baal, or the philosophical illusions of the present, they are found at the forefront of every civilization that has flourished on the planet. Egypt built pyramids to them, and medieval Europe burned them. Likewise, with the advent of the Age of Enlightenment Europe was shaken by them, and no concept of politics, art, or society is free from their influence. Occasionally, and usually at the cost of rivers of blood, man overthrows his illusions. However, in short order he comes to understand their necessity and replaces them with facsimiles. Without them we would not have progressed as a species, and without them we would soon return to our primitive, unthinking, barbaric state. As has been stated previously, it matters little whether the illusions refer to a concrete reality or to an abstract dream; they are real because we choose to allow their existence.

It may often be supposed that it is the intent of institutions of higher learning to shatter such illusions, to find fault and throw down those stories and oral histories upon which society has based its existence. By destroying the illusions, they destroy also the hopes and dreams of the people they portend to serve. On those occasions when such illusions are eliminated, collectives invariably rise in righteous indignation to oppose their attackers, usually to the great surprise of the supposed scholars. It is of no assistance to the learned that nearly all illusions have a greater or lesser basis of truth which makes their acceptance by collectives that much more unwavering.

To date, the great thinkers of society have produced few if any ideals which can charm the masses; as collectives must have their illusions at any cost, they turn instinctively to the speaker who offers them what they want. It is the lie rather than the truth which has most often developed nations, and for this reason many political systems retain a power which would evaporate under the light of an informed populace. Quoting Le Bon:

> *In spite of all scientific demonstrations [socialism] continues on the increase. Its principal strength lies in the fact that it is championed by minds sufficiently ignorant of things as they are in reality to venture boldly to promise mankind happiness. The social illusion reigns to-day upon all the*

heaped-up ruins of the past, and to it belongs the future. The masses have never thirsted after truth. They turn aside from evidence that is not to their taste, preferring to deify error, if error seduce them. Whoever can supply them with illusions is easily their master; whoever attempts to destroy their illusions is always their victim.[39]

The hard lessons of experience constitute the most effective process by which a truth may solidly established in the collective mind, especially if it runs counter to an illusion which has grown too dangerous to be perpetuated. However, singular experience is not sufficient to replace an illusion. The collective mind requires normalcy at all costs, as this is usually the most effective method of ensuring its survival. If an entrenched illusion grows to the level that it threatens the collective's health or very survival, the collective will often willingly march to its own destruction. Experience must therefore take place on a very large scale and be frequently repeated. A single shocking occurrence might be adequate to momentarily shatter illusions, but such illusions will be re-established quickly. Many striking experiences might very well be necessary before any real change comes to the collective mind, and even then the experiences may have to continue across generations before a truth takes final hold on the collective mind and soul. This is why historical facts, cited for demonstration, are generally ineffective agents for change. Their only real use is to prove to what extent experiences must be repeated from generation to generation to exert any influence, or to

---

[39] Gustave Le Bon, *The Crowd, A Study of the Popular Mind*

lend credence to argument against illusion.

For examples of this concept, one need only look to the recent historical record. Throughout the past hundred years many countries have given rise to democratic regimes which were not democratic. Ballot-box stuffing and voter intimidation was well documented and common, especially in poorer nations. Yet regimes which produced the illusion of democracy were better regarded by other democratic nations, even if their repressive leaders bordered on sociopathy. The title 'Democratic Republic' was enough to conjure images much different than reality, and through the *Principle of Inversion*, held more weight than the uncomfortable truth.

When discussing those immediate factors which might make an impression upon a collective, the subject of reason might be completely ignored if it was not necessary to point out the negative value of its influence. Through subtlety it might be used to influence a collective using reverse influence, but such an effort would require great skill and artistry. It has already been shown that the collective mind does not respond to reasoning, and can only comprehend simple chains of associated ideas. Rhetoricians who understand how to impress the collective mind appeal to them through use of emotionally charged images and abstractions. Standard logic has no effect on them.

To inspire a collective, a speaker must first completely understand the core prejudices and aspirations which give it unity. He must then pretend to share such sentiments and invoke them through basic associations and suggestive ideas. He must be willing and able to use tautology as a tool, and be able to comprehend any sudden changes to the emotional state of the audience. His language must change on demand, either to alter the mood of the audience or to react to it. For this reason, the best speeches are those which are delivered with the barest of outline. Prepared speeches are, as a general rule, much less effective.

The exception to this is the situation in which a speaker is required to underscore a striking occurrence, or a speech given to mark a leader's retirement. It has often been noted that concession speeches are quite often of such high quality that, had the candidate used such language during his or her campaign, such concession might not have been required. Leaders who have been forced to lead during time of war also have delivered many of the greatest of all remembered speeches. In such cases, the speaker understands that he is speaking not to a given collective but to history itself. He speaks for the collective which has followed him, and represents their sentiments to the future. At such times he appears truly a leader rather than an individual.

Le Bon adds a personal account of effective leadership of the collective:

> *"My first observations with regard to the art of impressing crowds and touching the slight assistance to be derived in this connection from the*

rules of logic date back to the siege of Paris, to the day when I saw conducted to the Louvre, where the Government was then sitting, Marshal V----, whom a furious crowd asserted they had surprised in the act of taking the plans of the fortifications to sell them to the Prussians. A member of the Government (G. P---), a very celebrated orator, came out to harangue the crowd, which was demanding the immediate execution of the prisoner. I had expected that the speaker would point out the absurdity of the accusation by remarking that the accused Marshal was positively one of those who had constructed the fortifications, the plan of which, moreover, was on sale at every booksellers. To my immense stupefaction--I was very young then--the speech was on quite different lines. "Justice shall be done," exclaimed the orator, advancing towards the prisoner, "and pitiless justice. Let the Government of the National Defense conclude your inquiry. In the meantime, we will keep the prisoner in custody." At once calmed by this apparent concession, the crowd broke up, and a quarter of an hour later the Marshal was able to return home. He would infallibly have been torn in pieces had the speaker treated the infuriated crowd to the logical arguments that my extreme youth induced me to consider as very convincing."[40]

Mathematical formulas, lines of reasoning, and statement of fact are no more convincing to a collective than

40 Gustave Le Bon, *The Crowd, A Study of the Popular Mind*

interpretive dance. The latter might even be preferable, as the entertainer is less likely to be murdered for his efforts. A speaker must understand that a collective retains both the power of a demigod and the reasoning of a child. No greater example of this is necessary than that offered by religious collectives. Despite the absolute lack of any evidence to support its ideas, the Heaven's Gate collective castrated itself, divested itself of all belongings, and finally committed mass suicide in preparation for a space ship it believed traveled with a long-period comet. Such devotion to dogma and illusion was and continues to be completely immune to any but the most rudimentary forms of reason.

Should it then be regretted that collectives are immune to reason? Reason would not have spurred humanity through successive plateaus of civilization. It was not leaps of logic but rather an immunity to logic which allowed 7200 men to stand for three days against the combined might of the Persian Empire (approx. 300,000 troops) at the Battle of Thermopylae—indeed, one must conclude that every rebellion against tyranny in the history of mankind began as a stand against reason. Every nation carries in its collective soul the accumulated memories of history, and it is these examples that it strives to emulate, even in the case of those examples which seem the most unreasonable. One might suspect that collectives are victims of the same forces which compel an acorn to transform into an oak or a planet to follow its orbit. It was improbable that Alexander, starting from such humble situation, would conquer the known world. It was equally improbable that a few bands of Arabs, emerging from the desert would conquer the greater part of the Graco-Roman world and establish an empire greater than that of Alexander. It was even more improbable that, hundreds of years later, an obscure and unknown French general would stride forward to bend nearly all of that same territory to his own will, or that centuries later a failed artist would rise to supreme leadership of a failed state and then build that same state into a war machine which nearly overcame Europe.

What little insight one might find into the forces at play in national collectives must be the result of pointed research into that nation's deepest history. The collective soul does not die. It gives birth to descendant collectives which carry its collective memory and character. If one accepts that a collective will revert to its character whenever it is allowed to do so, history becomes less a series of random chance and more a continuing process of self-actualization, intercourse, and disagreement by collective minds which continually evolve through interaction. History is not the story of the lone man. It is the story of the many who permitted him to lead.

Chapter IX: Leadership

"Authority doesn't work without prestige, or prestige without distance." – **Charles de Gaulle**

Many books have been written on the art of leadership, and any treatment of the subject within this text would be redundant. The effective qualities of leadership — foresight, understanding, and individual motivation, among others — would require such in-depth discussion that they would require a volume of their own. This book remains dedicated to its original subject: the collective, how it is born, its strengths, and its weaknesses.

Having given fair treatment to the mental qualities of a collective, and the motives which are capable of effecting the collective mind, it remains to describe how it may be set in motion and by whom such motion may be affected.

As soon as a number of living things are gathered together within a group with which they identify, they form a collective. Whether a flock of geese, a pack of wolves, or a pod of whales, or a crowd of men, they will place themselves under the control of a chief. Why should this be? Would it not seem more sensible that each individual creature within the collective would actively pursue its own best interests rather than that of the collective? Individuals within a collective gain more than

107

they relinquish, and as such is the case, self-sacrifice is often in the best interest of both the whole and the individual.

In the case of human collectives, the chief is often nothing more than a ringleader or agitator, but as such he plays an important role. If the mass of individuals within the collective represent the arms and body of the collective, the leader represents the brain. It is around his will that the opinions of the collective mind revolve. In return, he gains the full strength of body and purpose of the collective. Organization is necessary for a disorderly collective to evolve into greater order, and therefore greater depth of thought, and the leader represents the first stage along this path. If further subdivision is necessary within the collective, each such subdivision will have its own leader. This occurs whether they are chosen or simply rise to the need. Subdivisions of collectives are collectives in their own right, and will obey the laws and principles which apply to the larger collective. A collective is, after all, a herd of individuals which cannot intelligently move without a guiding shepherd.

The leader which is chosen by the collective—leaders rarely, if ever, choose themselves, although they may often present themselves well—will exhibit very special qualities which are needed by the collective. No two collectives being identical, each will have a surplus of a number of qualities and a dearth of several others. Whereas a gathering might be extremely well provided with willingness to fight, it may lack knowledge of effective tactics. In such cases an individual who exhibits tactical knowledge will rise to leadership. If the collective lacks philosophical ideology an agitator of an acceptable school of thought may be chosen. If it lacks funds for action, the leader who exhibits fund-raising knowledge may find himself deified. In all cases, a leader will have that which the collective lacks, and the collective will have what the leader lacks.

The leader may start as one of the led. He begins under the suggestion of a seemingly great concept or idea, and becomes its apostle. It takes possession of him as surely as if it were a spirit possessing his body—a fitting analogy as he is possessed by the soul of a different entity entirely. Depending on the depth of character within the leader, he may give himself to the idea to such a degree that other concerns vanish and every objection appears to him an error or a superstition. A leader of this nature (one arising from within a collective) may be classified as *internal leadership*, or a leader who is actively subservient to the collective he controls. To a large degree he is limited to the same conditions which limit the collective mind, and will serve only as a directing focus. He need not be gifted with keen foresight, nor could he be, as this quality generally lends itself to doubt and inactivity. Any foresight he had prior to his leadership is generally subdued to the collective will. He will generally rise from the ranks of the very nervous, the excitable, and the borderline delusional. However unlikely the idea he champions, his conviction is so strong that reasoning is lost. While he leads, he is invincible—persecution will not deter, derision will give no shame, and beatings will not dissuade, and argument will not be heard. He may sacrifice his friends, his career, and his family without concern. The sense of self-preservation is so subordinated that he may ask no more in reward than the opportunity for martyrdom.

In exchange for this, the strength of the internal leader's convictions gives the great power of suggestion to his words. Whereas an individual within the collective might shout and be heard by some few, the internal leader whispers and is heard by all. The collective is willing to listen to the strong-willed leader, who by nature understands how to impose himself upon it. The individuals within the collective have already willingly sacrificed their force of will to the greater purpose, and will turn instinctively to the voice which possesses the quality they lack.

Internal leaders often hold passable skill in rhetoric, although such is not strictly necessary. The collective will hear even a stumbling and dull speech as brilliant if the cause excites its imagination. However the internal leaders of history have almost always begun as individuals who have been fascinated by a particular creed: Peter the Hermit, Martin Luther, and Thomas Payne, and Eva Peron are excellent examples. They were able to call up in the collective soul that force known as faith, which renders men the slaves of their dreams.

The arousal of faith, whether religious, political, or social, and regardless of the object, has historically been the function of great leaders, and it is because of this that their influence has been strong. Of all the tools for shaping collectives, faith has always been the most striking—the Christian gospels correctly attribute to faith the capacity to move mountains. A man with faith is a force of nature, with the strength of ten men. The great events of history have been wrought by nameless believers who had little beyond faith in their favor. The great religions and empires of the world were not advanced through philosophy but through the fervor which comes from hope.

Internal leaders are plentiful when there is need. Every human contains within them the qualities necessary to become the object of popular adoration, regardless of whether they desire such attention or not. What internal leaders lack, however, is the objectivity of externalization. They have no power of calculation beyond that which the collective allows them. For this quality, a collective requires an *external leader*.

External leadership maintains the objectivity necessary to see multiple aspects of a situation and direct the collective accordingly. Generally, an external leader does not arise from within a collective but rather builds a collective around himself. He is part of the collective which he leads, but at the same time reserves a portion of himself away from the collective mind. He may initiate suggestion or contagion, but need not be subject to it. He gains strength from the collective will yet may resist its directives. Most importantly, he maintains the adoration of the collective so long as he represents to it the living image of its ideal. If such an ideal is shattered, he garners hatred equivalent to its prior love.

The external leader is normally part of a leadership caste, or a class of individuals to whom collectives normally turn for direction. He might be a congressman, a businessman, or an educator, or an entertainer. Like internal leaders, he will possess one or more qualities which is lacking in the subjected collective. He will additionally have a certain lack of empathy as to the needs of the individuals, as such concern would jeopardize his capacity to martyr his followers where necessary. Such leaders become presidents, dictators, and monarchs, tyrants, and generals.

External leaders must have at least a cursory understanding of the chain of communication between themselves and the followers. They represent the apex of a distribution network which extends from these powerful masters of men down to the common member of a collective who, in a smoky bar, slowly turns the hearts of his friends by ceaselessly drumming a series of simple concepts and catch-phrases which he barely understands. Such recruitment tools are generally made available through use of talking points, simple strategies, and leaflets, mass communication, etc. In such cases, the ideas originate from the external leader even if he later attempts to distance himself from their results.

In every class, caste, and community, as soon as an individual is not isolated he falls under the influence of a leader. Most men, especially within lower economic strata, do not possess clear and reasonable ideas on any subject outside of their immediate experience. The leader serves as their guide in this. The leader may be replaced by pundits and periodicals which provide talking points and ready-made arguments which remove the necessity for any thought on a given subject, although such mass-communication of direction lacks the power that a single leader's association holds.

Leaders, both internal and external, wield despotic authority. Such capacity for despotism is not only given, but it is required by the collectives they lead. They easily extort obedience from the most difficult of personalities. The reason for this is that while the individual feels the collective strength, he also understands that the leader might easily direct that strength against him. Such understanding demands acquiescence. It is external leaders which arrange strikes and decide pay-rates within unions.

These internal and external leaders tend to usurp the place of the public authorities whenever such institutions allow themselves to be called into question. Whereas collectives respect the despotic authority of their leaders, they despise the implication of leadership in others. In short order an institution such as a local police force might be stricken and replaced with members of the collective, if leadership feels such is possible. In such cases the dictatorial nature of the replacements ensure that the collective obeys their directives more docilely than their predecessors.

Regardless of those ideas around which a collective forms, it is not the need for liberty or freedom which binds it together; it is the need for the servitude which is a dominant characteristic of the collective. It is so bent on obedience that its membership instinctively submits to whomever declares himself the master. If for some reason a leader is removed from the collective, whether by arrest or loss of life, the collective does not necessarily cease to function. Initially the collective exists in a state of confusion and without any understanding of proper direction. However, in short order the collective will either elevate a new personality to the leadership or will disperse to reform with other similar collectives. In such cases, the new collectives gain the experience of the dissolved collective, and the collective soul is passed into new hosts.

Internal leadership generally possesses great energy, but only an intermittent strength of will. Internal leaders are normally violent, brave and audacious, and are generally most useful to direct sudden violent activities. They can generally be counted upon to carry spontaneous collectives with them in such enterprises, and when necessary will transform their followers from mere recruits into heroes within minutes. Such leaders, when divested of the leadership role, generally exhibit great weakness of character and individual willpower. Without conflict and great enemies against which to stand, they exhibit lack of self-direction and discipline. Such men make excellent leaders of the moment, and serve well in the capacity of transitory hero, but are usually ill-suited to be advanced to the ranks of external leadership.

External leadership exhibits enduring strength of will and greater foresight, often at the cost of energetic nature. Such leaders have a much greater influence. They are the founders of religions, and the leaders of successful corporations. St. Paul, Mohammad, and Christopher Columbus, Genghis Khan, and Benjamin Franklin are excellent examples of this category of leader. It is immaterial whether they are intelligent or narrow minded, as the world belongs to them. The persistent force of will they possess is a transmutation of the adoration of the collective—an immensely addictive and powerful faculty to which everything yields. Nothing resists it; neither nature nor man. This is the force of will which constructed the pyramids of Egypt, led the American Revolution, and built the railroads, and conducted two world wars. It is a power which lends itself both to explosions and slow fires, and when released can both build and destroy with equal utility.

When an individual wishes to sir up a collective for a short time, to induce it to commit an act of any kind, the collective must be acted upon by rapid suggestion, especially by a readily available example. Before this can occur, the collective should have been previously prepared by circumstances and the individual who wishes to lead must have demonstrated characteristics which the collective lacks. If, however, the collective is intended to exist for an indeterminate amount of time, other tools may be utilized. The most important of these are affirmation, repetition, and contagion. While their effect builds slowly, their results are lasting.

Affirmation which is kept free of any reasoning or proof is one of the surest methods of entering a suggestion into the collective mind. An affirmation with the least amount of demonstrable proof and the most concise form will be the most powerful in affecting the collective soul. Religious texts and legal codes of all ages have resorted to simple affirmation. Politicians call upon it to defend causes, and advertisers use it to sell products.

Affirmation, however, has no real influence unless it is constantly repeated, and as often as possible in the same form. At some point, the repetition raises the affirmation to the level of an abstraction, and through application of the *Principle of Inversion*, such abstractions become concrete reality within the collective mind. Consider the following affirmation: "*For every 1 mile per hour you reduce your average speed, you gain 1/10 miles per gallon.*" This affirmation, while generally accepted as true, is demonstrably false. Efficiency in a vehicle depends not on speed, but upon speed in relation to the vehicle's power-curve, which differs from vehicle to vehicle.[41] If a vehicle's engine and gear-ratio determine that it exerts the most power at 3500 rpm, then this will be the engine-speed at which, in any gear, it will get the greatest mileage. Such speed might be, depending on the differential, 73 miles per hour, 45 miles per hour, or 58 miles per hour. Such a simple concept may be easily proven simply through maintenance of a fuel record, yet the example affirmation was so often repeated in the 1970's that it is now accepted without question. The content of the affirmation was not of importance, so much as repetition of its content.

The influence of repetition on collectives is understandable when its power is seen in the influence of the most supposedly enlightened minds. The power is due to the fact that the abstraction of the statement is stored in

---

41 Irrespective of air viscosity, or drag. 'Drag' becomes a determining factor at speeds over 65mph, depending on vehicle design.

the collective long-term memory, where motivations for action abide. Eventually, the original author of the statement is forgotten, and the statement becomes an established fact regardless of content. To return to the previous example, the application of the *Principle of Inversion* becomes evident and its power proven. When members of the collective have heard the affirmation hundreds or thousands of times, they imagine they have heard it said in many quarters and end by establishing such abstractions as fact. "Why yes," they say, "I did notice that my fuel mileage increased when I began driving 50 miles per hour on the freeway." Even if their vehicle reduced its mileage, the reverse would be true to their minds.

Such methods are often used in electoral processes. If one candidate wishes to defeat another, it is rarely necessary to do more than repeat endlessly a simple fault of the opposition regardless of its truth. Eventually the statement will enter public conversation, be endlessly repeated, and finally cement itself as fact. The defense against this is, of course, to turn conversation from the supposed fault and to either an affirmation or a reversal of accusation—again through repetition. At worst, it will create confusion within the mind of the collective. At best, any emotional power set against the candidate will be turned against the accuser.

At times, it might be advantageous for a prospective leader to attack himself through use of allies. In such a case, the leader may address a known fault by use of occasional mention, and then combat it with much more powerful affirmation and repetition. In this manner, the possibility of weaponization of available fact or embarrassing indiscretion is removed from the opponent. An additional benefit is that such action lends the perception of power to the victor, which translates to a larger following.

When an affirmation has been repeated to sufficient degree, a public opinion is formed and contagion begins. Ideas, emotions, and beliefs have a contagious power within collectives more powerful than influenza. This is a natural phenomenon, and may be observed in animals when they are gathered together in groups. If a dog barks at a door each time any person passes, within days, every dog within the household will follow suit. In the case of men within a collective, emotions are rapidly contagious, which explains how seemingly unrelated events may cause a panic within a stock-market. Abnormal psychologists often must spend long hours in therapy if only to gain the upper hand on their acquired abnormalities. Such contagion may also pass between species, such as animals at a water hole which bolt at the first sign of fear, regardless of the presence of a predator, or between a nervous master and an excitable pet. The need of the individual to maintain unanimity with the collective is a basic aspect of nearly every species and might well be considered a sense on par with touch or smell.

For collectives to succumb to contagion they need not be present within a group, although such contagion is the most immediately powerful. Contagion may be felt across nearly any distance under the influence of mass communication, word of mouth, or simply knowledge of the same event. This is especially the case when the collective mind has been prepared in advance by remote factors. The example of the American Revolution has already been given in which for many long years dissertations on freedom and liberty were distributed through the relatively new publishing industry.

Imitation is, at its core, contagion put into practice. Direct communication was present but not necessary for the self-immolation of a single merchant in Tunisia to spread like an uncontrolled fire through the Muslim nations and topple well-established governments. Likewise, the changeable precepts of fashion provide excellent examples of contagion. The repurchase of clothing to conform to the shifting forms of fashionable society makes little sense from a practical standpoint, but from the perspective of the collective it is a natural extension of society. One would be brave to enter into a business meeting in 2010 wearing clothing in the style of the 1960's.

It is important to note that for imitation to occur between collectives, the collectives must have a commonality in regards to the action being imitated. If differences are too vast, such imitation cannot occur. Changes to the nature of a democratic collective, for instance, will likely not translate to imitation within a fascist collective. Across such vast gulfs, a common quality must first be established. Such qualities are the result of generational effort rather than sudden change, unless one collective or the other is overthrown and driven into utter defeat, as was the case with Japan at the end of WWII.

After the defeat of Japan by the United States in the

Pacific theater of WWII, the society of the island nation required rebuilding. This exercise was undertaken by US General Douglas MacArthur, who wielded near dictatorial authority over the newly forming society. Japan had already modernized to the point of industrialization, and so it was not so great a leap for the nation to also adopt a parliamentary democracy as a form of government. Following the restructure, Japan became one of America's closest allies.

Contagion is so powerful that it forces upon the individuals within a collective not only certain opinions, but modes of feeling as well. It is the cause for the contempt in which such works as "Lady Chatterley's Lover" were held, as well as such movies as "The Last Temptation of Christ." However, years past their much disputed arrival, both of these works received acclaim from many of the same individuals who had decried them years earlier.

The opinions and beliefs of the collective mind are propagated by contagion but never by reasoning. Those concepts which cycle through membership of the lower economic classes are acquired at bars and union-halls as the result of affirmation, repetition, and contagion. There is little difference between the methods used to propagate the concepts of socialism and the methods used by nascent Christianity. It should be noted that contagion, after having been at work among a lower economic class, will spread to a higher economic class. Such continues to occur with socialism, and will likely occur with whichever grand idea arises to replace it.

Through an understanding of this process, one may trace the path of travel of ideas from conception, to contagion, and finally to universal acceptance. The idea begins as a concept raised by a small collective intellect or an individual. This idea is communicated, usually through print, to others of the same social strata. After it has been dissected, distilled, and reduced to some semblance of acceptability, it is simplified and offered to the general populace. At this stage, the idea may be quashed without much effort through use of affirmation, repetition and contagion. If, however, the idea is not quashed, it begins to be slowly repeated throughout the lower economic classes of society. Leaders and agitators who have dedicated themselves to the service of the idea embrace it, distort it, and create a collective cult which further distorts and spreads the message. Once this process has begun, it can be slowed by the same methods mentioned above, but it cannot be stopped. The idea will take root so long as there are those who are willing to chant its mantra. Eventually, it will be grasped as a concrete truth by a great enough number that it leaps to members of the next higher economic rung. Through the same process, the idea plants itself, takes root, and if the ground is fertile enough it blossoms. The cycle repeats itself until generations later the idea has permeated every level of society from the impoverished to the hyper-wealthy. At this stage the idea, regardless of its merit, becomes a popular truth. At this transformation the idea has the greatest chance of implementation by its disciples, especially if they are led by a member of the external leadership. If this is the case, action may take any course from internal debate to armed conflict, depending on the idea. At this point, the strength of the parent collective is gauged. If it can survive the change, it will continue to grow. If it cannot, it must either destroy the challenging collective or fall.

As has already been stated, a collective will seek out the strongest leader, and will choose that leader which best represents the qualities it lacks. Le Bon called this quality 'prestige', and that label is as good as any other. Prestige is the quality which provokes awe or fear. It demands acquiescence, and even when martyrdom is required it leaves the expectation of reward. Further, it is able to do these things without any additional effort by the leader in question. An accurate definition of **prestige** might be, *the quality of an idea, person, or object in which it may be viewed both as concrete and abstract simultaneously.*

What then is the source of this ephemeral quality called prestige? Many dissertations have been written on the subject, but rarely if ever do such texts discuss the subject from the perspective of collective dynamics. Through application of the various laws and principles of collectives, one may come to understand those laws and principles which define natural-born leadership. One may further understand that leaders are rarely born with the necessary qualities. Such qualities must be earned through sweat equity.

Prestige requires, at its outset, some semblance of power. Such power may derive from organizational position, family name, or past victory, or association with another leader who exhibits prestige. This initial concept of power gives the prospective leader the capacity to take leadership of an initial collective. From that point forward, accumulation or loss of prestige occurs based upon the leader's capability.

It is perhaps appropriate, having thus far categorized and defined other aspects of collectives and their leadership, that this text categorize the various forms of prestige. They may be reduced to two principle varieties: associative prestige, and situational prestige. Associative prestige is the weaker, but may be acquired by any individual regardless of character. A purchased title, acquired wealth, or proper uniform are fine examples of associative prestige. Situational prestige, however, derives from the physical characteristics or personal accomplishments of the leader in question. This is by far the most powerful form of prestige. Situational prestige may be acquired, but only by way of victory. The commander of victorious troops, the talented entertainer, or the brave explorer are examples of individuals with situational prestige.

Prestige need not be associated with an individual. The concept of democracy bears its own prestige, which it lends to such institutions which call themselves democratic. Likewise, the church maintains a high degree of prestige. Perhaps the greatest level of prestige possible is that of association with God, or Divine Right. Such prestige has allowed children to lead without question from the deep recesses of history. Prestige which is associated with a concept or institution lends itself well to individual leaders, but it may be withdrawn too easily for it to be relied upon as anything other than initial prestige.

Prestige of either kind, regardless of its nature, allows the individual or concept to be both concrete and abstract at the same time, as stated in the previous definition. It is the effect of creating a cloak of abstraction about an existing object such that it never appears to the collective as it truly is. When prestige is lent to a specific enterprise, the quality translates as if the enterprise has already succeeded, regardless of its nature or intent. If the enterprise comes to fruition, the prestige from the success is redoubled and returned both to the originator and the results of the enterprise. If the enterprise fails, the prestige is lost until success occurs in another arena.

Consider the statues of Easter Island or monolithic Stonehenge. Both locations enjoy great levels of prestige. If one were, however, to come across either of these locations without knowledge or understanding as to their supposed reverence within society, one would find dilapidated statues in the former case and a crumbling stone-age construction in the latter. Neither would likely be sufficient to give rise to any more than the most transitory curiosity. Through the eyes of the greater human collective, however, the statues of Easter Island and Stonehenge gain the abstract qualities of being both unknown and unknowable. Their very dilapidation adds an aura of mystery which can only increase their prestige.

This quality may be increased through success and the previously mentioned methods of repetition and affirmation. Affirmation alone is sufficient to create prestige in the case of entertainers, a fact well used by the large movie production houses of the early cinema. Companies such as Warner Brothers and MGM made good use of both mass-media and the press to laud the quite often fictitious qualities of their star actors, which translated to box-office sales.

Used together, the various forms of prestige might be well-nigh overpowering. Consider the following example. A prospective leader enters the military collective and through effective use of tactics and motivation achieves several victories and a respectable rank. This person could claim a greater-than-average level of prestige. If that same person were to then leave the military and enter the world of education, achieving the status of President in a respected university, he would have achieved great prestige. Finally, if that same prospective leader used his prestige to solicit the funds necessary for a bid for political power, he would be a devastating force with which to reckon. Such an individual, buoyed by first situational prestige, then acquired prestige, and the vast power of affirmation and repetition, would be nearly assured eventual election in a democratic nation. Such a person would also be known as Dwight D. Eisenhower, popularized by the affirmation, "I like Ike."

Another example of the multiple use of prestige to acquire power might easily be given in the meteoric rise of President Obama. Taken by himself, President Obama would have been an extremely unlikely candidate for President of the United States. His initial success in politics came not from acclaim, but by virtue of the fact that he eliminated his opposition before any voting could occur. His position in the State Assembly of Illinois garnered him a small amount of power and a modicum of prestige. Through distribution of well written auto-biographies and association with prestigious members of the Democratic Party, he gained further prestige. Finally, through excellent delivery of rhetoric and skillful use of both media and a second-to-none activism machine (ACORN) he secured the nomination of the Democratic party for President of the United States. Against an opponent whose prestige derived from service as an officer in the U.S. Navy and a tradition of 'maverick politics', his overwhelming victory was unsurprising. What was truly surprising was that through the entire journey he resisted calls to prove his citizenship, never released his college transcripts, never authored a popular piece of legislation, voted infrequently on the legislation of others, never completed a full term of office at the national level, and suffered through very limited negative campaign tactics by his own party. His lack of experience or evidence of prestige was overwritten by the projected abstract image of success, correct or otherwise, which bore greater weight than any prestige which could be arrayed against him.

Any numbers of factors can be utilized in the generation of prestige; but success is one of the most important. Every successful individual, every idea that forces itself into the collective mind, ceases to be called into question. The proof that success is chief in the generation of prestige is that when the former disappears, so too does the latter. The hero of today may well be the villain of tomorrow if he is visited by failure. Additionally, the dislike afforded him will be directly proportional to the acclaim he received previously. Prestige fades slowly, and represents an emotional potential. If that potential cannot be directed positively, it will be directed negatively. Quoting Le Bon:

> "Believers always break the statues of their former gods with every symptom of fury. Prestige lost by want of success disappears in a brief space of time. It can also be worn away, but more slowly by being subjected to discussion. This latter power, however, is exceedingly sure. From the moment prestige is called in question it ceases to be prestige. The gods and men who have kept their prestige for long have never tolerated discussion. For the crowd to admire, it must be kept at a distance."[42]

---

42 Gustave Le Bon, *The Crowd, A Study of the Popular Mind*

Chapter X: The Abode of the Martyr

"It is the cause, not the death, that makes the martyr." –
Napoleon Bonaparte

Ideas are the abode of the martyr, and represent the
fuel with which a collective may undergo movement and
growth. Some ideas are immutable, the result of eons of
adaptation and reinforcement. Such concepts are as in-
grained as genetic code, and may be changed only
gradually over time. Other ideas are as variable as an
animal's coloring, and may change from generation to
generation. As with a breeder who controls mating to
generate an ideal of outward presentation, such ideas may
be manipulated to generate desired results. Alongside the
unalterable soul of a collective are changeable elements
which may be altered. For this reason, one will normally
find a fixed groundwork on which are erected edifices of
sand. While the daily tide of fate might erase the work of a
single day, the foundations remain little changed.

The ideas of a collective are categorized into two
separate classes. First there are great permanent beliefs,
which endure for several centuries, and on which
civilizations are built. Good examples of this category
might be feudalism, Christianity, and democracy. Such are
the nationalist principles and social ideas which dominate

nations today. Second, there are transitory, changing opinions. These are as prone to reversal as fashion, and may be demonstrated by the practice of political polling. Ideas are like the motion of a deep river; while ripples might dance across its surface, the general motion and track of the river remains largely unchanged.

The great permanent beliefs are few in number. Their ascendancy and fall marks the culminating points of the history of every race, and they constitute the real framework of civilization. It is comparatively easy to successfully suggest an acceptable transitory idea to a collective, but extremely difficult to implant a permanent belief. However, once established, the permanent belief is as difficult to uproot as it was to establish. It is normally changed only at the cost of violent revolution, and even then is as likely as not to be reinstated after the violence ceases. Revolutions generally succeed in their purported purpose only when an idea has almost entirely lost its influence on the collective mind—the beginning of any successful revolution is the end of a belief.

The exact moment at which a permanent belief is doomed is easily recognized; it is the moment when its value begins to be called into question. Every permanent belief is little more than a widely accepted fiction; it can only survive on the condition that it is not critically addressed.

Even when a permanent belief is shaken, the

institutions to which it gives rise retain their strength and disappear slowly. When the belief has completely lost its influence, everything that was built upon its foundation is quickly lost to ruin. No civilization has yet changed its founding beliefs without simultaneously transforming the elements of its civilization. Such a civilization must continue the process of transformation until it has found and accepted a new permanent belief, and until this point it is in a state of anarchy. Permanent beliefs are the pillars of civilization; they are capable of inspiring faith, and creating a sense of nationalism and duty.

Nations have always been conscious of the necessity of acquiring permanent beliefs, and have understood that the loss of the same would be a trumpet call which signaled their decline. In the case of the Roman Empire, the cult of Rome was the belief which allowed them to conquer the world, and when this permanent belief was allowed to die, so too was Rome allowed to cease its preeminence. After the fall of Rome, it was only after Europeans developed new commonly held permanent beliefs, namely the concepts of monarchy and Divine Right, that they were able to gain the cohesion necessary to claw their way from anarchy. It is not simply obstinacy which causes a nation to show intolerance in defense of its opinions. This intolerance is the lifeline of a people who cannot survive without their foundations.

This intolerance deserves treatment within this text, because it is a necessary extension of any organized collective. Just as a man will starve and die when separated too long from food, so too a nation withers and dies when its central ideas fall into question. It was to found or maintain permanent beliefs that so many were sent to the stake in the Middle Ages, and that so many philosophers and inventors have died in despair and disgrace even if they managed to escape martyrdom. It is in defense of such permanent beliefs that so many wars have been fought and so many good men killed in the past two hundred years. A nation is in itself a permanent belief, an abstraction which is in turn supported by other abstractions.

Permanent beliefs, as has been previously stated, are difficult to establish; once they have taken root, they become invincible. Regardless of how false they might be from an intellectual standpoint, they will flower as a concrete truth in even the most enlightened minds within a collective. In biblical account, the practice of burning one's children in the hands of an idol to Moloch was one of the widest and most accepted practices throughout the Middle East, even though such practice was so horrible that loud singing and music was necessary to drown out the screams of the victims. That the practice sacrificed the very future of society did not matter; in the mind of the greater human collective of the time, Moloch was as concrete and real as any potentate. Nothing is more hypnotizing than the effect of permanent beliefs, but at the same time nothing can better mark the humiliating limitations of human intelligence. As soon as an acceptable permanent belief is planted in the collective mind it becomes the source of inspiration from which institutions, arts, and civilizations develop. The influence it holds over the collective mind is absolute. Internal leaders live to realize the belief, legislators to apply it, and philosophers, artists and writers to be preoccupied with its expression.

From a fundamental permanent belief other transient opinions rise, but they mirror in some way the permanent belief which gave them birth. The Egyptian civilization, the European civilization, and the Muslim civilization of the Arabs are the result of a small number of permanent beliefs which have captured the collective soul, and leave marks which are immediately recognizable.

This is why, thanks to permanent beliefs, individuals of every age are categorized by the network of traditions, opinions and customs which gave them similarity, and from which prison they could not escape. Men are guided, before anything else, by their beliefs and by the customs which spring from the beliefs. These beliefs and customs dictate the most minuscule acts of our existence, and even the the most individualistic of individuals cannot claim independence from their tyranny. The tyranny of the collective mind is the only real oppression, because it cannot be killed. Tiberius, Genghis Khan, and Napoleon were tyrants, but from their graves Moses, Buddha, and Jesus, and Mohammad have exerted a far greater despotism. While violent revolution may overthrow a tyrant, how can it overthrow the willing subjugation of the soul?

The absurdity which often marks permanent beliefs has not stopped their acceptance. Rather, the preeminence of a belief seems to require some level of mysterious absurdity, in order that it might gain mystic acceptance. Because of this, the weakness of socialist beliefs gives them credence rather than acting as an impediment to their spread. The true weakness to the belief in socialism is that, unlike the religions it wishes to supplant, it does not offer eternal happiness in a later life. Rather, it offers happiness through social equality, a condition which must eventually be held to popular judgment. Its strength can only increase until the day in which it is implemented, at which point the belief is subject to discussion and eventual revolution.

Upon the fertile ground of permanent belief is found an overlying growth of opinions, ideas and thoughts which are constantly growing and dying as they compete with each other. Some might exist for a day, while others might grow and live for a generation. The changes which cause such transitory beliefs are more superficial than real, and they are always affected by the collective soul. The varying preeminence of one party or another in national discourse is an excellent example of shifting beliefs. So long as the party in power is successful, it enjoys the prestige of such success and control of the collective. If the collective in question meets with defeat or disaster, regardless of cause, the party loses such prestige and may lose power to a political rival.

In the absence of any intellectual or philosophical test, it might be supposed that collectives change their transitory beliefs at will, and such supposition is supported by history. Collectives do not act in a random manner, however; a collective will adopt those transitory beliefs and customs which seems to it most appropriate at any given time, based on its perceived needs and such qualities as it lacks. As has previously been stated, tyrannies exist not because of the overbearing willpower of the the leader, but because of the desire of the led. Leaders do not belong to themselves, and are as much servant as master.

If, in the course of history, a large collective finds itself with a surplus of those commodities necessary for life, it will adopt a more liberal outlook towards society and grow until it has reached such a point that consumption meets production. If thereafter sudden conditions change the availability of commodities--a drought or sudden attack by a rival collective, for instance--the transitory customs and beliefs will shift to a more conservative mindset. Once parity is again attained the collective may at its leisure be either liberal or conservative, as influences continue to dictate. This is the grand dance of the collective; it is necessarily chaotic as it exists in a chaotic universe.

If one were to closely examine the transitory beliefs of a collective, he would note general characteristics. Those that are found in opposition with the permanent beliefs and sentiments of the collective soul are short-lived, and the diverted stream soon resumes its course. Transient opinions which are not linked to any permanent belief, and which cannot then possess stability, are at the mercy of every change in circumstance. As they are formed by suggestion and contagion, they are necessarily momentary; they rise and fall as rapidly as waves upon an ocean excited by wind.

Some factors will allow the greater or lesser propagation of transitory beliefs. Primary among these factors is a decline in permanent belief. As has already been stated, a collective must be formed around a centralized idea. If the idea is shaken, it will struggle to find a new, more stable idea. The weakening of a permanent belief is much the same as the tilling of a field: it clears the ground so that other, more transitory beliefs may take root.

The second factor is the power of the collective. In repressive regimes, collective power is centralized around a single individual or group of individuals. Such collectives have very little internal structure other than that necessary for survival, and are therefore much more resistant to change. If multiple collectives are allowed to exist within the same framework, however, transient beliefs may rise and fall as the collectives interact and trade thought-images amongst themselves.

Finally, the power of mass media is a driving factor in the propagation of transitory beliefs. The same newspaper or news network may present wildly contradictory news and opinion content, which once presented to a collective either takes root or not depending on the prestige of the presenter and the predisposition of the audience. Given an audience which is heterogeneous, the suggestions which result from each individual opinion are soon overwritten in the collective mind by a competing suggestion. As a consequence no opinion becomes widespread, and their existence has little effect. If, however, the media maintains a more homogeneous audience, the presented opinions might be considered to carry great weight and might persist for a significantly longer time.

As a result of these factors, one must conclude that governments are, as a whole, powerless to control public opinion. The idea that a given mode of media might sway opinion, especially given the vast number of choices available to the average consumer, is a false idea. As the success or failure of a pundit or presenter is dependent upon the viewership they might inspire, their opinions necessarily must be the reflection of current transitory beliefs, rather than the initiator. If a conservative news outlet gains suddenly in popularity it is not the work of the producers, but rather a shift in the nature of the overall audience which has caused it to be so. Just as likely, the same news outlet will lose viewership to more liberal venues when conditions have changed.

Perhaps the least effective method, politically, of retaining power is the individual interview. The interviewee supposes that his ideas and opinions, as presented, might sway the populace to his general support. The interviewer supposes that the prestige of his position either supports or destroys the prospects of the subject. Neither is correct. The interview serves to solidify the politician's image in the mind of the electorate, and forces him to defend positions in the future which he might otherwise more wisely oppose. Perhaps the true value to such interviews is the opportunity to build a less defined image to which the collective may assign mystical importance or the definition of choice. Beyond this, the practice is useless. Quoting Gustave Le Bon:

> *"Become a mere agency for the supply of information, the press has renounced all endeavor to enforce an idea or a doctrine. It follows all the changes of public thought, obliged to do so by the necessities*

of competition under pain of losing its readers. The old staid and influential organs of the past, such as the Constitutionnel, the Debats, or the Siecle, which were accepted as oracles by preceding generation, have disappeared or have become typical modern papers, in which a maximum of news is sandwiched in between light articles, society gossip, and financial puffs. There can be no question to-day of a paper rich enough to allow its contributors to air their personal opinions, and such opinions would be of slight weight with readers who only ask to be kept informed or to be amused, and who suspect every affirmation of being prompted by motives of speculation. Even the critics have ceased to be able to assure the success of a book or a play. They are capable of doing harm, but not of doing a service. The papers are so conscious of the uselessness of everything in the shape of criticism or personal opinion, that they have reached the point of suppressing literary criticism, confining themselves to citing the title of a book, and appending a "puff" of two or three lines."[43]

As a result, the following of public opinion has elevated itself to the status of a reality show, wherein experts are called upon to dissect every piece of legislation, every speech, and each political occurrence as it happens. The validity of such commentators is largely a matter of faith, as a public opinion poll is valid only for the moment in which it was taken. What might be widely supported

[43] Gustave Le Bon, *The Crowd, A Study of the Popular Mind*

today might easily be the source of derision tomorrow. This absence of direction of opinion, taken concurrently with the ongoing dissolution of permanent beliefs, has as a result that collectives tend to be disinterested in anything which does not directly affect their interests. As a result, commentary on current affairs is generally the purview of professional rhetoricians whose success or failure depends more upon their pithy commentary than upon accurate interpretation. Such is to be expected within the current collective dynamics, and is neither good nor evil.

The general wearing away of permanent beliefs by the constant action of waves of transitory sentiment should not be too greatly mourned. It is a symptom of the decadence of a collective. Men of great insight and genuinely strong conviction exert a far greater force than men who deny, criticize, or are indifferent. It must not be forgotten that if a single opinion were to gain sufficient prestige to enforce its general acceptance, it would soon have such tyrannical strength that everything would bend before it and conversation would cease. It is for this reason that the slow accumulation of prestige for permanent beliefs and the quick accumulation and loss of prestige for transitory beliefs continues to function effectively in society. While the collective might prosper under the short-term benefits of transitory beliefs, the longer-term benefits of the permanent belief will continue to allow them cohesion and meaning. Nations that fall under the power of the collective do not live long lives.

Chapter XI: Differences of Type

"Science is the systematic classification of experience." – **George Henry Lewes**

Up to this point, this volume has been concerned with the general nature of collectives and how they may be expected to develop. As with all other subjects of study, collectives may be better understood if they are categorized into their most common forms. In this way their actions might become more understandable, and their direction more accurately predicted. Each category of collective has its own typical characteristics and is therefore to a greater or lesser degree predictable.

The most basic form of collective is the family unit. It is the base material from which collectives draw their constituent units, and defines as well as any other factor the underlying belief system and propensity towards action. Family units are composed, preferably, of a leading personality, a supportive personality, and one or more developing personalities. Without any of these three aspects the family collective must adapt by fulfilling the role in other respects. A family without children may adopt, or may take in animals which fulfill the developing personality role. A family without a supportive personality may divide the duties among itself or replace the role with an outside personality. A family without a leading personality will either adapt by choosing a new leader within its ranks or will turn to a suitable father-figure to acquire stability. Tribal societies are especially comprised of this basic form of collective and little more.

Above the family collective is the disorganized collective, or a collective comprised of dissimilar elements which identify with a common goal or idea. Within such collectives the only commonality is the bond of the collective will to achieve a purpose, and such characteristic is usually personified in a chief or captain. A platoon of soldiers or horde of barbarians is categorized in this fashion. Also of this nature are organized collectives, or collectives comprised of similar units. Such collectives generally form around a permanent belief and regulate themselves through use of dogma. Organized collectives cannot consider themselves to have a supreme leader because the dogma and the permanent belief fulfill that purpose. Rather, organized collectives have leadership which is subservient to the permanent belief. A priest caste is an excellent example of such a collective.

Above the disorganized and organized collectives is the super-collective, or the collective of collectives. The super-collective allows individual collective minds to interact in a relatively safe environment, and through the interaction develops that depth of personality which is generally equated to a national identity. Additionally, super-collectives allow instability of the individual between collectives, which is extremely important to a collective's development. Historically, repressive regimes, caste systems, and rigid social strata have resulted in stagnation and mere survival, while more liberal regimes and open societies have resulted in the greatest developments. This is because of application of the *Principle of Imprint, Principle of Inversion*, and the *Laws of Contagion and Mental Unity*. When an individual moves from one collective mind to another (and an individual may be a constituent within several, simultaneously) he does more than change the nature of his submission. The *Principle of Imprint* ensures that the images of the previous collective's thought processes remain indelibly imprinted on his mind, and further experience will be colored by their understanding. Upon admission to the new collective, the new images of the new collective mind's thought processes become imprinted as well. From this point, having the perspective of two separate minds, the individual is free to develop new associations between the collectives. Through application of the *Law of Contagion* such new concepts spread through the collective at the speed of available communication and have the opportunity to be discussed. Finally, if a large enough portion of the collective accepts the images as valid, the *Law of Mental Unity* will ensure that all members of the collective gain the impression of the concepts. This process increases in effectiveness when newsletters or other forms of mass communication allow the use of affirmation and repetition. In this manner, for good or ill, simply with the addition of new membership a collective may be unalterably changed. Such change eventually must change the super-collective of which it is a constituent.

Disorderly and orderly collectives may, under certain influences, be forced to exchange natures. Orderly collectives might devolve to disorder, and disorderly collectives might suddenly find a unifying permanent belief.

Until this point, disorderly collectives have been the subject of this text. They are composed of individuals of any description, of any profession and with any degree of education or intellectual ability.

Simply because men form a purposeful group, they become a part of a new organism and contribute to the collective mind. Their individual natures subvert, and their personalities take on those qualities which are common to all. Reason holds no sway, because the new collective mind maintains no capacity for such concepts. It is entirely directed by the unconscious motivations of the individuals, and the soul of the parent collective allows that the newly formed collective may be predictable in some ways. A collective composed of only Englishmen will differ in many ways from a collective composed of several nationalities, by virtue of the effect of the English collective soul over the former. In the latter, the wide divergence in the underlying nature of the individuals cancels out any influence such national soul might exert. An example of this is best found in the United Nations, where individuals under the influence of vastly different national souls attempt, poorly, to craft world-wide policy. The collective state is a barbaric state if not directed by some overarching set of social mores, and with the controlling permanent beliefs which define a national soul the collective is freed from a degree of barbarism.

The only further classification necessary to be made of disordered collectives is to separate them into either anonymous collectives such as street mobs, and non-anonymous collectives such as congresses and juries. The main difference between these two types of collective is that in the former there is little sense of responsibility, whereas in the latter the constituent member retains responsibility for his actions. Juries are as unlikely to commit rapes and murders as street-mobs are unlikely to demand evidence before sentencing.

Orderly collectives include sects, castes and classes. The sect represents the first step in the process of organization of ordered collectives. A sect includes individuals who differ greatly as to their education, professions, and class of society, and maintains cohesion through common beliefs. An example of this type of collective would be a sect of Christianity, or a political party. The caste is the highest degree of organization which a collective is susceptible. While sects include individuals of different persuasion, the caste is composed of individuals of the same profession, and therefor of similar education and social status. An example of this would be a trade union, a military caste, or a priestly caste. Finally, a class is formed of individuals of various origin who gain cohesion by economic status, habits of life, and/or level of education. The middle class and peasant class are excellent examples of this concept.

When two or more collectives join together to form a

combination analogous to a family unit, they become a super-collective and gain access to higher levels of collective thought. Super-collectives in general attempt to fulfill, on a larger scale, the same roles which are necessary in a family unit. One collective generally leads, one supports, and other nascent collectives are spawned from the association. As these proto-collectives develop, they gain capacity from each of the parent collectives and therefore greater depth of collective thought. This is the only way in which any collective might claim any level of internally conscious direction.

Eventually, if the super-collective continues to exist and develop, it will develop its own collective soul. From that point forward, the soul will determine the character of individuals within the subordinate collectives. Also at this point, curiously, the collective will spontaneously develop a leadership caste. This leadership caste, while subject to the collective soul, remains separate from the collectives they lead. Such leadership castes are important in that they allow the collective to move and grow with the forethought of overall survival, regardless of the survival of the individual constituents. The nature and sentiments of the leadership caste generally reflects those qualities lacking in the super-collective as a whole. It should also be noted that the immortal words of Lord Acton apply especially to a leadership caste: *"Power tends to corrupt, and absolute power corrupts absolutely. Great men are almost always bad men."*[44] It is perhaps because of this truism that leadership castes appear to progress in parallel to criminal collectives.

---

44 Lord Acton, in a letter to Bishop Mandell Creighton in 1897

Chapter XII: Criminal Collectives and Juries

"I was married by a judge. I should have asked for a jury." – **Groucho Marx**

Because collectives, after being temporarily influenced, enter into an automatic and unconscious state in which they are guided by suggestion, it would appear difficult to qualify them as either upright or criminal. The reason for the inclusion here is the influence of criminal gangs and organized crime. Certain acts of collectives may be considered criminal, if considered by themselves, but criminal in the same way that a cat toying with a mouse might be considered criminal. The usual motive for the crimes of a collective is suggestion, and the individuals who assist in such crimes are afterward convinced that they observed duty. Such is not the case with typical criminal behavior.

The concept of crimes against humanity falls into this category. In cases of this sort, a trial eventually devolves to a leader's claims that he performed his duty as it was revealed to him, for the good of the collective. In general, such defense is not accepted. What is not considered is the effect of the collective mind, will, and soul upon the leader in question. It is very possible that a leader, having identified too strongly with the collective of which he is a part, might fall victim to the illusions of strength and anonymity and the *Principle of Inversion*. In such cases, the collective mind holds sway rather than the individual intellect. This is a danger inherent in leadership, and a reminder to the prospective leader to maintain a sense of detachment. Certainly the activities which are to be deliberated by juries, in such cases, might legally be crimes; to call them pathological, however, would be incorrect. A fine example of an individual who committed crimes under the influence of the collective will would be the much-celebrated case of Patricia Hearst.[45]

Criminal collectives will have in general the same characteristics as disorganized crowds: credulity, suggestibility, and instability, the exaggeration of emotion, and the manifestation of the morality of the parent collective. Consider an example from American history, that of the mafia. The Mafia had, as its parent collective, the soul of Sicily. As such, it existed as a collection of crime families whose organization supported respect for internal authority, survival, and profit. Although the Mafia did not give homage to the same judicial system which ruled other members of society, it maintained an internal system of justice which was as swift and final as any the United States might provide. Laws were not necessarily codified, but they were understood: pay your debts, tell no one, obey orders,

---

45 Patricia Hearst was the granddaughter of the rich and powerful publishing magnate William Randolf Hearst. Ms. Hearst was kidnapped by the Symbionese Liberation Army, and was absorbed into their collective as the first diagnosed case of 'Stockholm Syndrome'. She was later convicted of assisting her captors in a bank robbery.

protect the family, etc. When motivated to action, the criminal collective is ruthless and final. As survival of the collective is paramount, the practice of murder and brutality loses its stigma. In all, such collectives are amazingly strong and may be finally overcome either through such thorough extermination that no seed of its existence may be passed to a new generation, or by absorbing them through social osmosis into one or more larger, more acceptable collectives. Both remedies are the work of generations, rather than the outcome of single efforts.

Juries represent the capacity for either great justice or great injustice, depending upon how they are used and how they are influenced by circumstance. Being unable to examine every category of jury, this text will examine the most important: juries of criminal cases. In addition to these are professional juries, congressional juries, and the like. Such juries respond to much the same influences as criminal juries, but with other motivating factors.

Juries provide excellent examples of non-anonymous disorderly collectives. They have as leadership a judge who directs them in methods, and their collective will is marshaled to perform a specific action: judgment. They display suggestibility and slight capacity for reason, yet are open to the influence of legal professionals from both sides of a criminal proceeding. Finally, they are guided by the collective unconscious, which lends credence to subjects of emotional power. They are influenced both by contagion and by the *Principle of Inversion*, but the *Principle of Imprint* plays little part. Such a gathering of individuals is supposed to be less likely to commit errors of judgment, yet one will see that such errors are equally likely if control is not maintained by the presiding judge.

The decision at which a jury must arrive is simple in nature, which is appropriate for a collective. The arrival at a decision of either innocence or guilt is the totality of their purpose. As such, images which relate to innocence or guilt must be the tools used to sway their opinion. A defense lawyer who argues along lines of solid reasoning might reasonably prove that his client was not the perpetrator of a murder, but if the prosecutor of a weak case chose instead to focus on the horrific nature of the crime the defendant would be as likely to be found guilty and condemned to prison. Such is the nature of collectives that the emotional argument will succeed where the intellectual argument will not.

Juries represent a special case, in that the specific purpose for the collective is known in advance and the participants are largely voluntary. Individuals within the jury have the capacity to maintain a reflective distance from the collective mind and may, through suitable self-control, maintain individuality. On non-specific questions such as character, however, the collective will give greater weight to abstractions than to concrete evidence. As such abstraction holds greater reality than the evidence in question, character becomes an important subject in both defense and prosecution.

If a jury is required to understand technical data, the results of scientific tests, or complex formulas, however, one might just as well employ a panel of chimpanzees. Collectives cannot, as a whole, comprehend the complex. Attempts to force them to do so will result in either anger or disinterest. In such cases the collective will attempt to perform its stated action without reference to technical data. From Gustave Le Bon:

> "For instance, a gathering of scientific men or of artists, owing to the mere fact that they form an assemblage, will not deliver judgments on general subjects sensibly different from those rendered by a gathering of masons or grocers. At various periods, and in particular previous to 1848, the French administration instituted a careful choice among the persons summoned to form a jury, picking the jurors from among the enlightened classes; choosing professors, functionaries, men of letters, etc. At the present day jurors are recruited for the most part from among small tradesmen, petty capitalists, and employees. Yet, to the great astonishment of specialist writers, whatever the composition of the jury has been, its decisions have been identical. Even the magistrates, hostile as they are to the institution of the jury, have had to recognize the exactness of the assertion." [46]

Juries will regardless be comprised of individuals who form a collective, and such individuals will, under the effects of the collective will, pursue the ideal of justice with

---

[46] Gustave Le Bon, *The Crowd: A Study of the Popular Mind*

the same zeal as a crusading knight or willing martyr. In such respect, the lawyers on either side of the contest should strive not so much to select jurors whose sensibilities lean toward their client, but rather to select jurors whose sense of detachment might lead them to differ from the collective will. Such individuals might be convinced to deviate from the collective opinion where a true believer would willingly submit to it and consider it his own.

As they are collectives, juries are impressed by emotional suggestions. They will readily respond to an individual whose appearance evokes a desire for protection, while they will tend to look poorly on individuals whose bearing brings to mind frightening images. That women rarely are sentenced to a death penalty, regardless of their innocence or guilt, should be proof enough of this quality.

Juries may be impressed by prestige, but use of prestige runs a risk of the prestige being turned against its wielder. When the popular entertainer Martha Stewart was placed on trial for insider trading, her prestige was of no avail. Rather, upon repeated insistence as to her rude behavior, jurors found her guilty and left the courtroom saying, "It was a victory for the little guy." That none of the 'little guys' were improved in any way mattered not at all. The vitriol brought about by the shattering of her public image was all that was necessary for sentiments to be turned against her.

The turning of sentiments within a jury does not

require a lawyer to to convince all members of the jury; he is sufficed to convince those individuals who dominate through personality. Such personalities will, through contagion, spread their opinions to others within the collective.

One might conclude that juries are ineffective, but such conclusion would be inaccurate. Juries represent the final line of defense for innocent individuals to avoid punishment for crimes they have not committed. A judge or magistrate might find an individual guilty based on circumstantial evidence and a desire for public vengeance. With a jury there is at least the possibility for a defendant to convince his peers of his innocence. An individual accused of high crimes is not placed before a jury unless one or more judges has already concluded that the case has enough merit to continue. Such a defendant is better served by a jury than by a judge whose sentiments will necessarily lend more weight to a prosecuting attorney. A jury alone exists in a capacity which cannot be replaced by an individual. It alone can temper the severity of a law which should, by definition, be equal for all.

Chapter XIII: Congress and Death

"A democracy which makes or even effectively prepares for modern, scientific war must necessarily cease to be democratic. No country can be really well prepared for modern war unless it is governed by a tyrant, at the head of a highly trained and perfectly obedient bureaucracy." – **Aldous Huxley**

Parliamentary or congressional collectives present the same qualities as other non-anonymous collectives. The only restraint to which they respond is the possibility that their actions might have consequence. Although the method of their election might differ from country to country, and the control of the collective soul might differ between peoples, they tend to have very similar characteristics. The collective soul will allow characteristics to be weakened or exaggerated, but will not prevent their manifestation. Finally, although the nature and rules of those debates held by various congresses and parliaments might differ, the nature of their voting trends remains the same. In all, one form of deliberative body is equivalent to the next.

Congresses represent the current ideal of civilization. The system is the expression of an idea that a large gathering of men is more capable than a small number for the purpose of making wise decisions on any given subject. A cursory examination of the basic laws and principles of collectives will show this to be a false assumption, but congresses generally adopt circumventions to allow both the illusion of deliberation and the effectiveness of decisive leadership in matters of legislative concern. This text will limit itself the the United States congress, which is a largely transparent entity and therefore easier to study.

Simplicity in opinion and thought is one of the most important characteristics of congresses. The overwhelming collective principles at hand render even the most complex of issues apparently subject to simplistic and short-sighted solution. Monetary concerns which cannot be forestalled will be either ignored, delayed, or treated with an indifference to budget which would cause the average businessman to blush. Abstract principles, especially if they do not apply to the question at hand, are the solutions of choice. Naturally principles will vary with party representation, but due to the fact that the members are a part of a larger collective, they are inclined to exaggerate the worth of their principles and direct them to the extremes of acceptability.

Extremism in elected officials is often lauded by a constituency. Popular leadership, even if it is ineffective leadership, demands at least the appearance of a permanent belief around which a constituency may gather. If such a belief does not exist, the congressperson must 'fake it', giving the appearance of passion where disinterest exists. Thus one may see an elected official vigorously pound his fist upon a podium in defense of a seemingly innocuous piece of legislation, yet completely overlook a more important bill which might have benefited from his attention. Those true believers who from time to time achieve office must carefully tread the path between fanaticism and intellect. While fanaticism is not necessarily anathema to sound judgment, it is often turned against the fanatic when action is required by a political enemy. In such cases where skillful use of rhetoric and situation raise the emotional state of an electorate, a fanatical representative opposes the constituency at his own peril-- even if such opposition is of greater benefit to the people than obedience.

Congresses are directed by suggestion, and, as is the case with all collectives, the direction originates from those leaders who possess prestige. Such suggestibility, however, has its limitations, which it is important to note.

On questions of local or regional legislation members of a congress will have firm and likely unalterable opinions. The direct order of even a prestigious party leader would likely have little effect upon a congressperson whose constituency demanded a new road, a better bridge, or funding for the local police. The suggestion of the constituents on items of direct and local interest generally outweighs the suggestion of local leadership. In these matters, their combined prestige outweighs any which is held by an individual member of the congressional collective.

On general questions such as the imposition of a tax or the assignment of funds to a particular national project, any surety of opinion vanishes and the prestige of leadership plays a large role--although not the same way as in a disorganized anonymous collective. Each party has its own leadership which possesses occasionally equal influence. The result is that the representative finds himself caught between two contrary suggestions, and is given pause to hesitate. Even if given the opportunity to ponder a question solely as an individual, the pressures brought to bear by a large congress invariably will swing a vote in one direction or another.

It is a misconception that fear of reprisal from a constituency on such national matters will weigh heavily upon a representative. Such fear might exist somewhere in the back of his mind, but if he has spent any length of time in his position he will understand that unpopular votes might involve backlash, but only for a very short period of time. As a general rule, the character of a representative mirrors the requirements of a constituency. He will exhibit those qualities the constituency lacks and represent such permanent beliefs as the constituency holds dear. As soon as the representative is able to vote in a different session, and in agreement with the constituency, any backlash which has not faded will disappear. The constituent collective is no more capable of memory than any other collective, and will react to the most recent stimulus.

Regardless, it is the party leaders who maintain mastery in discussions of national import. The need for these leaders is necessary as they are found in congresses and parliaments in every democratic nation, and function as the true leaders. Men within a collective demand leadership, so it is the result that votes within a congress actually represent the wishes of a small minority of leaders, a very few individuals who break with their party, and such independent representatives as may hold office in that given term. The influence of the leaders is due in small part to the arguments they offer, but to a large degree to the prestige their powerful positions provide. The best proof of this is that, if for any reason their prestige is lost (such as in the case of scandal), their influence disappears. Their prestige is individual, and can only be re-accumulated through use of methods which require more time than is available in such sessions.

A collective would immediately lose its characteristics if it were to credit its leaders with the services they render, and a congress is no different. A collective which obeys a leader is under the influence of his prestige, and its submission is not dictated by self-interest or gratitude. Because of this, a leader with enough prestige may wield almost absolute power.

One should not harbor grudges against congressional leaders. Regardless of whether their leadership is enlightened or dull, they represent the will of the greater super-collective. As such they are the physical embodiment of the collective will, and must react to such or fail in their positions. A leader is rarely very far ahead of public opinion, and his actions often represent a conflict between that which he knows is right and that which he is forced to do at the behest of his large constituency. In cases where the two are in direct conflict, the constituency will almost always be victorious. Memory of his deeds may quickly fade, but anger at supposed betrayal fades much more slowly.

With the understanding that a congress or parliament is little different than any other collective, the manner in which congressional leaders wield their power should become obvious. First the leader must have at least an intuitive understanding of the dynamics of collectives, and must know how to speak to them. He should be aware of the imagery which all members of the congressional collective hold in common, and understand how to call powerful emotions to mind through use of words, phrases and images. He should address the assembly through use of strong affirmations--devoid of any proofs--and impressive images, alongside very simplistic arguments. In such a way a leader within a congressional assembly may exert his will on the collective as a whole.

In the case of any leader, but especially within a congress, the demonstration of intelligence often creates more harm to his cause than good. Intellectually, one might suppose that intelligent argument is to be lauded in the high deliberative bodies of a nation, but the reverse is true. If a congressman is intelligent and highly educated, and chooses to show the complexity of issues by explaining and promoting comprehension, he will be seen as indulgent and will blunt the intensity of conviction necessary to lead. The great leaders of collectives have not required great intellect. Instead, great passion and conviction are most useful to a leader of a collective of any size.

It is not lamentable that strong leadership favors

those of strong conviction and narrow mind. Such is necessary for a man to ignore obstacles and display strength of will. Collectives instinctively recognize men of energy and conviction, and turn to them for the masters they require.

In the face of such an understanding of collectives one might despair at the use of such governing bodies as parliaments and congresses. Such bodies would have quickly failed as governments if they were not able to circumvent many of the difficulties surrounding collective decision making. Bills are not, generally, written by congressmen. Especially considering the length and complexity of many bills, the congressmen either employ teams of office personnel to write the bills or receive them pre-written from lobbyists or think-tanks. Such bills generally include a synopsis (which may or may not be representative of the bill) from which simple arguments might be formed. Other representatives also read the synopsis and form their opinions based on its content. Deliberation proceeds, and the bill is passed or failed--*often without any member of congress ever having read its contents*. In cases of national emergency a congress generally accedes to the will of the national leadership, and thus need not formulate any plan which requires forethought. In all, this particular system of government allows for slow movement in any direction. If a direction of travel is deemed by the national leader to be unhealthy, he can redirect the congress by direct leadership or by popular acclaim. Quoting Gustave Le Bon:

"In spite of all the difficulties attending their

working, parliamentary assemblies are the best
form of government mankind has discovered as
yet, and more especially the best means it has
found to escape the yoke of personal tyrannies.
They constitute assuredly the ideal government at
any rate for philosophers, thinkers, writers, artists,
and learned men00in a word, for all those who
form the cream of a civilization." [47]

It is important to note the two inevitable outcomes of a parliamentary or congressional government: waste, and progressive loss of freedom. The first of these is the consequence of a lack of foresight within collectives. If a member of a congress proposes a measure to extend the pensions of state workers, or to provide for the needs of orphans, no other member of congress would likely dare vote against it. It would matter little if the programs which provided for state worker pensions and orphans were already over-funded. It would be impossible for them to hesitate to give their votes, because the abstraction of starving, homeless orphans would far outweigh the concrete reality of a thinly stretched budget. Additionally, the consequences of debt are remote while the consequence of voting against orphans would likely haunt them in re-election. In addition to this, there is the importance of voting affirmatively on grants for local works. A congressman can only ensure that expenditures within his district are met if he also agrees to vote for other local expenditures.

The second of the previously mentioned dangers is

---

47 Gustave Le Bon, *The Crowd: A Study of the Popular Mind*

the inevitable restriction of freedom which is the natural result of parliaments and congresses. Such is the result of the innumerable laws, always restrictive, which congresses consider themselves bound to vote and to whose consequences they are blind. Congressmen themselves likely do not comprehend the pit into which they lead their constituencies. As a congressman, an individual is expected to pass legislation for the good of their districts, and legislation never expands freedom. Eventually in the life of any parliamentary system some method of erasure must be enacted so that the growing elephantine legal code might be reduced in size to the point that it may be read by a single individual in less than a lifetime, but such methods do not currently exist.

There is an additional danger associated with congressional governments, one which is not so readily foreseen--that of encroaching bureaucracy. Each law and regulation is not in itself an end, but a direction which must be obeyed. With each law comes the requirement that public servants be employed to oversee its application, and further public servants to manage the process. Initially, such bureaucracy is limited and effective, but as bills are proposed and passed it necessarily becomes more extensive. Presidents and prime ministers might provide visible representations of a government, but it is the bureaucracy which stamps the passports, issues the visas, issues the licenses, and inspects places of business. Eventually in any congressional government the bureaucracy will expand to the point that it becomes a collective unto itself. When this happens, the collective will of the bureaucracy holds great power and great prestige, but without direct collective leadership. If such a power were to gain such leadership, control of the country might easily be wrested from the congress and permanently instilled in the bureaucracy--an institution which is notoriously inflexible, intolerant, and dictatorial. The administrative caste is the only portion of government which does not change, and it is alone in possessing irresponsibility, impersonality, and perpetual existence.

Between the accumulation of laws and the growth of the bureaucracy, the result is the confinement of the citizen within narrower and narrower limits of freedom. Eventually the citizen tires of struggling against the yokes of government and ends by wishing untroubled servitude. Then all spontaneity and energy is lost, and they are no more than the passive, unresisting and powerless automatons of their faceless masters. Quoting Le Bon:

> "Arrived at this point, the individual is bound to seek outside himself the forces he no longer finds within him. The functions of governments necessarily increase in proportion as the indifference and helplessness of the citizens grow. They it is who must necessarily exhibit the initiative, enterprising, and guiding spirit in which private persons are lacking. It falls on them to undertake everything, direct everything, and take everything under their protection. The State becomes an all-powerful God. Still experience shows that the power of such gods was never either very durable or very strong. This progressive restriction of all liberties in the case of certain peoples, in spite of an

outward license that gives them the illusion that
these liberties are still in their possession, seems at
least as much a consequence of their old age as of
any particular system. It constitutes one of the
precursory symptoms of that decadent phase which
up to now no civilization has escaped." [48]

This, then, is the end of all things and the doom to which any and all nations may look forward. It is the lesson of history and the future of mankind. It seems inevitable that all peoples should pass through the same phases of existence, as history has so often watched peoples follow this same course. A study of every great and eventually failed civilization will inevitably find the same path traveled by all. At the dawn of their birth, men of various origin are brought together by chance, invasion, and conquests. Of different races and creeds, the common bond they hold is the law of their chief. They form a collective from necessity and exhibit all the classic manifestations of the same: the heroism, the weakness, and the impulsiveness, and the violence. Nothing about them is stable, and they are rightly called barbarians.

Eventually, time accomplishes what revolution and deep thought cannot: the association with surroundings, the repeated intermarriage, and the necessities of life commonly effect necessary changes. The collective of unlike individuals blends into a whole, to form a people--that is, a gestalt which possesses common characteristics and a

---

48 Gustave Le Bon, *The Crowd: A Study of the Popular Mind*

common national soul. This people is able to emerge from barbarism, but will only emerge completely when it acquires a permanent belief, or ideal. The nature of the ideal matters not at all; whether it is the cult of Rome, the might of Athens, or 'Liberty and Justice for All', it is enough to give all of the individuals within the nation perfect unity of thought. At this point they become a civilization, with all the institutions, beliefs, and arts which are born from the same. In pursuit of the permanent belief this new civilization acquires all the qualities it requires: splendor, vigor, and grandeur. Eventually, the civilization reaches its peak. From that moment forward it begins the inevitable slide towards destruction from which neither gods nor men escape. It has ceased to grow, and is therefore condemned to a speedy decline.

This moment is marked by the weakening of the permanent belief which once gave it unity. As this ideal loses prestige, all the religious, political, and social structures which it inspired begin to shake. As the ideal is progressively dismantled, the people loses more and more of its identity, its vigor and its strength. The intelligence of the individuals may increase, but the same time the soul of the nation is supplanted and the capacity for collective action is undermined. What was once a people becomes in the end a group of disconnected individuals, held together for a time by crumbling institutions and traditions. At this stage men, divided by interests and aspirations, incapable of self government, require that they are directed in their slightest acts. The State exerts an absorbing influence.

With the loss of the old ideal, the soul of the race

disappears; it is no longer a people, but a swarm of individuals and it returns to its original state. Without consistency and a future, it has all the characteristics of a disorganized collective. Its civilization is without stability, and is at the mercy of random chance. Barbarism mounts. Eventually, even the crumbling edifices of civilization must fall to reveal the rot which began at inception, and the people is no more. Quoting Le Bon: *"To pass in pursuit of an ideal from the barbarous to the civilized state, and then, when this ideal has lost its virtue, to decline and die, such is the cycle of the life of a people."*[49]

---

[49] Gustave Le Bon, *The Crowd: A Study of the Popular Mind*